277)

Katherine Muir
Newcastle
22. 6. 79

Speed Memory

My special thanks are due to Heinz Norden for his permission to use the Skipnum Memory System and for his extensive help morally and editorially, and to my personal assistant, Joy Buttery, for her encouragement and perseverance.

Speed Memory

Tony Buzan

David & Charles
Newton Abbot   London
North Pomfret (Vt)   Vancouver

ISBN o 7153 7365 X

Library of Congress Catalog Card Number 76-40809

Previously published in 1971 by
Sphere Books Limited

Set in 10 on 10 pt. Plantin
and printed in Great Britain
by A. Wheaton and Co. Exeter
for David & Charles (Publishers) Limited
Brunel House   Newton Abbot   Devon

Published in the United States of America
by David & Charles Inc
North Pomfret   Vermont 05053   USA

Published in Canada
by Douglas David & Charles Limited
1875 Welch Street   North Vancouver BC

297,195

TABLE OF CONTENTS

RECALL AND LEARNING

This chapter will explain how your memory works while it is actually learning, after it has learnt something, when it is particularly trying to remember something, and when it is using special memory techniques.

Recall during a Learning Period

In order for you to see clearly how each human mind does recall things, it is useful for you to experience recall during learning yourself. In order to do this, follow these instructions carefully: below you will find a long list of words. Read the list, one word at a time once through only, *without going back over any word*. The purpose of your reading the list is to see how many of the words you can remember. The order does not matter. It will be impossible for you to remember *all* of the words, so when you are reading the list, simply try to remember as many of them as you can. Start reading now:

Was
Away
Left
His
To
And
The
Far
Of
And
That
The
Of
Beyond
Leonardo da Vinci
Which
The

Must
And
Of
Could
The
Range
Of
And
Else
The
Walk

Now that you have completed that list turn to page 18 where you will find questions relating to your recall during learning.

Your individual score may have varied slightly from the general average, but it should have demonstrated the normal performance of recall during a learning period.

Virtually without exception, people remember more of what they learned at the beginning of a learning period, slightly more of what they learnt at the end of a learning period, much more of things that were associated, and always those things which in some way are outstanding.

Thus the words which are commonly remembered in the test given are those at the beginning of the test, 'away', 'was', 'left', and 'his', one or two of the words at the end of the list: 'walk'; those words which were associated in some way, for example 'the', 'and', and 'of' (words associated by repetition); and those words which are outstanding in this particular example 'Leonardo da Vinci.' In addition people will sometimes remember words around the outstanding word, simply because those words are associated to it.

As significant as those things which are remembered, are those things which are *not* recalled. In other words, anything which is not at the beginning and end of a learning period, which is not associated to other parts of the learning in some way, and which is not outstanding, will tend to be forgotten. In many cases this means that the entire middle bulk of an amount to be learned is forgotten.

Next, ask yourself the following question: if you had been studying a difficult text for forty minutes, had found your understanding poor throughout, and had noticed that during the last ten minutes of your reading your understanding had begun to improve considerably, would you either: stop your studying immediately, pat yourself on the back and conclude that as you had started to do well you could now stop; or would you carry on, assuming that now that your understanding was flowing more smoothly you would be able to keep it going until it trailed off, and *then* take your break.

Most people choose the latter of those two alternatives, assuming that if their understanding is going well other things will be going well also.

It can be seen from the results of this test, and from your own personal experience, that recall and understanding are *not* the same. They vary in their performance as time progresses. All that we understand we do not necessarily recall, and as time progresses we will recall less if we do not in some way solve the problem of the large dip in recall (see graph) that occurs during the middle of a learning period.

What we must try to do is to make the recall and the understanding work in harmony. And we can only do this by organising the time during which we learn in such a way as to make understanding high without giving recall a chance to sag too deeply in the middle.

It is therefore necessary to break the learning period up into the best time units. The best time units, for most people, turn out to be between twenty and forty minutes, as shown in the graph on page 10. If the time is organised in this way, a large number of advantages become apparent:

1. Each of the individual dips in recall during the learning period is not so deep as if the person had carried on without the break.

2. Instead of only two high points of recall at the beginning and end of the learning period, the person who has properly broken up his time has eight relatively high points of recall.

3. Because of the breaks, the person taking them will be far more rested during the next learning period than will be the person who is "slogging through" without a break. The advantage here is that when a person is rested both recall and understanding function more easily.

4. Because the person who has taken breaks is both more rested, and is recalling more of each learning section, his comprehension of the new section in which he finds himself after the break will be greater.

9

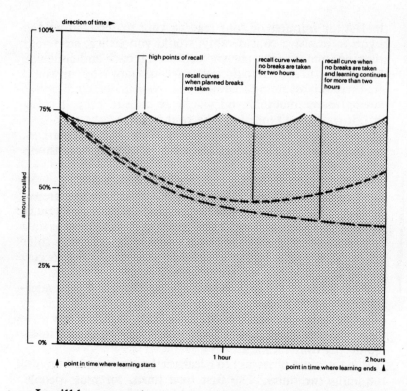

direction of time ►

high points of recall

recall curves when planned breaks are taken

recall curve when no breaks are taken for two hours

recall curve when no breaks are taken and learning continues for more than two hours

100%

75%

50%

25%

0%

amount recalled

1 hour

2 hours

point in time where learning starts

point in time where learning ends

It will be greater because he will be recalling more of what went before, and will therefore understand more of what he is currently reading. The person who has not taken the break, in addition to his fatigue, will not be recalling so much of what went on before, and therefore will not be able to make so much sense out of the new information he is tackling.

5. Contrary to 'commonsense' your recall of what you have learnt *rises* during a break rather than beginning to trail away. This rise is due to the fact that your brain 'sorts things out' for a little while after you have finished taking in information. Therefore when you return to your learning after the break you are actually in possession of more knowledge than if you had carried on without the break. This last piece of information is particularly important, because it helps get rid of the guilt feeling that many people have when they find themselves taking a break and thinking that they ought to be getting 'back to the grindstone'.

The breaks should usually be no longer than two to five

minutes. During the break you should allow your mind to rest, by either doing light exercise, making yourself a non-alcoholic drink, or resting. You should not watch the television, start to read magazines, 'phone friends, or engage in any activity which will enable you to carry on making excuses for not returning to the task at hand!

If you organise your learning in this way, your recall of any material you learn will improve very noticeably.

At the beginning and end of each twenty to forty minute learning period, it is advisable to do a very quick review of what you know to that point in time, as well as a quick pre-view of the material you are going to cover during the next learning period. This continuing review pre-view helps consolidate the information you already have, gives you confidence as you progress, and allows your mind to get a 'bird's eye view' of the territory it is going to have to explore during its next learning period.

Recall after Learning

Once you have made it easier for your recall to work well *during* a learning period, it is important for you to do the same thing for your recall after the learning has finished.

The pattern of recall after learning, often called forgetting, contains two 'surprises': first, you retain more of what you have learnt *after* a few minutes have passed since the end of your learning period; second, you lose 80% of the detail you have learned within twenty-four hours of having learnt it!

The rise is beneficial, so you want to make use of it; the decline can be disastrous, so you need to make sure that it does not happen.

The method for both maintaining the rise and preventing the decline is *Review*. Review is best done in the following manner:

If you have been studying for one unit of time, the high point in your recall after learning will occur approximately one tenth of a unit afterwards. For example, if you had studied for an hour the high point in recall would be approximately six minutes after you had finished learning. This high point is the ideal time for the first review. The function of your review is to imprint the information you already have in your mind, in order to make it more 'solid'.

If you manage to review at the first high point, the graph of recall after learning changes, and instead of dropping the detailed information, it is maintained for approximately ten units of time. So for example, if you had studied for one hour your first review would take place after six minutes, your second review would take place ten hours later.

From then on your reviews should take place only when you feel the information is perhaps slipping away. These reviews on average will take place over units of time which are each four times as large as the previous time. So, you might review after one day, then after four days, then after sixteen days, then after forty-eight days, then after ninety-six days, and so on.

[Each review need take very little time.] The first one should consist of a complete reviewing of your notes or information after the learning period, and may take as much as ten minutes for a one hour learning. After the first review, each subsequent review should consist of a quick jotting down of the basic information in your area of interest, and then a comparison of your quick note with your basic notes. Any areas you have left out can be filled in, and any new knowledge you may have acquired during the period between reviews can be added to your original notes. In this manner your recall of all the information that you need to have constantly available can be guaranteed.

In order to emphasise the importance of continued review, it is useful to compare the mind of the person who does consistently review, with the mind of the person who does not. [The person who does not review is continually putting information in, and letting that same information drain out. The person will constantly find it difficult to take in new information, because the background knowledge he needs to understand that new information will have gone. In such a situation learning will continually be difficult, recall will always be inadequate, and the whole process of learning, understanding, and recalling will be unpleasant and arduous.]

The person who *does* review will find, that with the constantly available store of increasing information, new information will slot in more easily. This will create a positive cycle in which both learning and understanding and recall assist each other, making the continuing process increasingly easy.]

Surprisingly, the more you learn, the more easy it is for you to learn more. It is similar to the biblical phrase 'to him that hath shall be given, and from him that hath not, even that which he hath shall be taken away'.

This information on recall after learning can also be applied to our current attitudes towards the decline of mental abilities, especially memory, with age. All our current statistics indicate that as human beings grow older their memories become increasingly worse after the age of 24. These findings, substantial as they seem, contain a major fault. They are based on surveys carried out which studied people who generally did not have any information about how their memories worked, and who consequently tended to neglect them. In other words, the tests showing that human memory declines with age were performed on people who consistently did not review what they had learnt, and who therefore fell into the second category of the biblical statement.

* Recent tests on people who have begun to review suggest that the opposite of the established trend is in fact the case. If the memory is continually fed and nurtured it will continue to improve with age. The more that is fed to it the more it has to associate to other areas of knowledge, and the more it will be able to 'link' various pieces of information with all the others. Thus the ability of the human mind to remember will increase until the last few days of a person's life, as long as it is looked after.

Your Retention—Could it be Perfect?

The preceding sections have shown you how to develop your recall ability during a learning period and after a learning period.

Memory is composed not only of recall, the ability to 'get back out', but also of retention, the ability to 'put in'. If it is possible to continually recall more and more, how much are we actually able to store? Recent evidence indicates that our retention may indeed be far in excess of what we had previously thought it to be.

The following are simply a few of the areas suggesting our increased capacity:

1. *Death-type experiences*

Many people, having come face to face with death, explain that in the split second when they 'realised that this was it' their entire lives stretched before them. In such instances, for example coming face to face with a sixty-mile-per-hour lorry, or falling off a cliff top, the split second in which the person 'realises' the situation seems to expand into infinity, and the entire experience of the person's life is reviewed on an 'inner eye'. The experience is not uncommon, and those questioned insist that it was not simply a series of highlights, but an entire re-run of their life to date. Explanations put forward include the following: that during the shock second of realization, all connections within the brain are made at once, and a complete and instant review of everything is seen.

2. *Possible physical inter-connections in your brain*

Professor Anokhin of Russia has estimated that the number of physical inter-connections possible in the average human brain is: 1 followed by ten and a half million kilometres of type-written noughts! Professor Anokhin stated that the ability of the human mind appeared to be unlimited as far as his knowledge of its physical make-up went.

3. *Dreams*

Many people experience dreams in which they recall or dream of people and events from many years ago. These people and events have often been 'totally forgotten' until the time of the dream, and yet when they are dreamt they appear in 'full and perfect clarity'. The fact that *some* items such as this, which had been 'forgotten', can re-appear with such clarity, suggests that there may be many other such stored images, people and events waiting for their turn to re-appear.

4. *Surprise random recall*

Virtually everyone has had the experience of turning a corner and suddenly recollecting people or events from previous times in their lives. This often happens when people re-visit their first school. A single smell, touch, sight, or sound, can bring back floods of experiences which it had been assumed were forgotten. Once again this ability of a given sense to bring back perfect recall, suggests that if there were more correct 'trigger situations' much more would be recalled, and therefore also suggests that the brain *has* retained it.

5. *Penfield's experiments*

Professor W. Penfield, of Canada, found that when he

stimulated different parts of the brain with tiny electrodes, the brains that he was stimulating recalled events from all periods of their lives. The outstanding feature of their recall, was that *everything* was recalled. Penfield checked with relations and acquaintances of the people he had been working with, and found that their recalls *were* as accurate as they had suggested, and not only that, but that the recall seemed to be a total re-living of the previous experience. This suggested to Penfield that the human brain photographed, like a comprehensive movie camera, everything that it was paying attention to at any given time. Penfield suggested that with the right stimulation any event from a person's past life could in fact be brought back to the present.

6. *Rosensweig's experiment*

Professor Rosensweig, who has experimented on the interconnections between the individual cells of the brain, has estimated that if we fed in ten new items of information *every second*, for an *entire* lifetime, we could in no way fill the capacity of the human mind.

7. *The Russian 'S'*

'S' was a Russian journalist whose editor observed that during briefing meetings at the newspaper, 'S' would take no notes. After some embarrassing questions, in which it turned out that 'S' could see no *reason* for taking notes, it was discovered that he recalled everything. 'S' was immediately put in contact with the Russian psychologist Professor Luria, who proceeded to do a long series of experiments with 'S'. It was confirmed that 'S' could in fact remember virtually every event from his life, going so far as to be able to remember complicated formulas, of which he had no basic knowledge, over a period of sixteen years. There have been other famous 'natural memorisors', who suggest, by their ability to recall everything, that the mind can certainly retain everything. It was confirmed that the minds of these amazing memorisors were fundamentally no different from the minds of other human beings.

8. *Language*

In our day to day use of language, we 'forget' the extraordinary memory ability we use to speak. Every time you speak, your mind is instantaneously recalling every word that you use, and also those words that are spoken to you. We do not continually interrupt conversations asking people to pause while we recall the various words that they are using. We recall instantly. In fact the process is a matter of micro-second timing, well beyond the ability of even the most sophisticated computer.

9. *Mnemonics*

The last piece of evidence for the possibility of our retentions being perfect is the ancient art of mnemonics. Mnemonics were special memory systems devised for remembering items that were not normally connected. It is these techniques which form the bulk of the remainder of this book.

Mnemonic Techniques

Mnemonic techniques or memory systems are based on the simple principles of association and imagination. In these techniques the idea is to connect the object or idea you wish to memorise with an object or idea that is already 'fixed' to a standard memory system.

The two ideas, the fixed key-word, and the one you wish to remember, have to be linked or associated in the most imagina-tive manner possible. This is done by blending things with each other, hanging them off each other, smashing them into each other and so on. The blended images must be as imagina-tive as possible, so that all possible senses can be brought into the imagined link-up. The more immediate the linkage is, and the more senses that can be brought into the image, the more definitely will it be recalled.

Until recently these techniques had been thought of as gimmicks or tricks. It is now recognised that the techniques are in fact based on the basic principles by which we normally do memorise; which are association and the awareness of our multiple senses.

In fact if one studies even the simplest mnemonic technique (see pages 27–33), one can see that the process is in fact very akin to creative thinking. Creativity is often defined as the ability to link two images that previously were unlinked in such a way as to form an imaginative, exciting and new image. Both memory and creativity can then be seen as different

16

aspects of the same process.

The function of memory systems can therefore be seen not only as enabling you to remember specific things you wish to remember, but also as systems, which if used, will enable your mind to develop its creative facility.

In addition, studies done by Professor Ornstein in California, have shown that the right side of your brain, which is usually under-exercised in traditional Western education, *needs* to express its imaginative, colour, and rhythmical abilities. Practice using mnemonic techniques enables exactly this kind of freedom.

Finally, it can be seen that the memory techniques have a far wider range of application than simply a one-up-manship at social gatherings. The techniques outlined in this book will enable you to confidently improve your memory in a large range of areas, as well as giving your mind the opportunity to expand its creative and linking ability.

Your memory really is better than you think.

The outlook of this book is a positive one, and will attempt to counteract the current trend towards assuming that our memories are really not that good, and that computers can do much better.

CHAPTER ONE

MEMORY TEST

Few people ever put their memory to the immediate test, and it is for this reason that most are unaware of the limits and habits of their mind's work.

The tests that follow *should* not be too difficult, but because of the way we are trained (or not trained!) in school, the simple tasks you will presently attempt will in some cases prove very very difficult and in others almost impossible.

Do not worry about poor performance, since it is the purpose of this book to make the memorisation of all items in the following tests an easy and enjoyable exercise.

Looking at this situation from a positive point of view, the more difficulty you experience now, the greater will be your improvement by the time you have completed this book.

LINK TEST

Read the list of 20 objects once through, and then immediately cover it or close the book. On a separate piece of paper write down as many of them as you can remember, attempting to get them in the correct order.

Score yourself in two ways: first the number of items you remembered out of 20, and second, the number of items that you listed in the correct order (if you reversed certain items they are *both* wrong with regard to the second score.).

Cup
Shop
Chimney pot
Judge
Suitcase
Toe
Mountain
Star
Couch
Ice cream

18

Jail
Spoon
Book
Spider
Scissors
Plant
Nurse
River
Stain
Mongrel

Score: Number remembered ....

Number in correct
order   ....

PEG TEST

Give yourself no more than four minutes to remember this second list of 20 items. The aim in this test is to remember the items in random order, connecting them to their appropriate number. When four minutes have passed cover the list or close the book, write the numbers from 1–20 on a piece of paper, and fill in the answers randomly, that is, pick a number on the list and fill in the item which belongs to that number. Do *not* progress regularly from 1–20. Jump about all over the numbers until you have filled in as many as you can. And still another don't: *don't* mumble through the list each time in order to get a number—pick it out of the air!

1. Tar
2. Aeroplane
3. Leaf
4. Shell
5. Hair
6. Moon
7. Lever
8. Lighter
9. Railway
10. Field
11. Atom
12. Wheel
13. School
14. Sand
15. Doctor

16. Spectacles
17. Lake
18. Feather
19. Sock
20. Pump

Score: Number correct ....

FACES TEST

Look at the 12 faces on the following two pages for not more than four minutes, then turn to the end of this chapter where the same faces are presented without their names. Try to match the right name to the right face. Score one point for each correct answer, and *take off* one point if you fit a name to a person of the wrong sex!

NUMBER TEST

Look at the four 15-digit numbers printed below, giving not more than one minute to each. At the end of each two minutes close or cover the book and write down the number as best you can, giving yourself one point for every number that you put down in the correct place.

936811475298694
937943271621487
689223841378534
543712298374973

Score: 1 .... 2 .... 3 .... 4 ....

TELEPHONE NUMBER TEST

The following is a list of 10 people and their telephone numbers. Study the list for not more than five minutes, then close or cover the book and write down first the name and then the numbers. Give yourself 1 point for each correct number (even if you make only one mistake in the number you must consider this totally wrong, for if you had dialled it you would not have been put in contact with the person with whom you wished to speak!)

Your local butcher	329–8737
Your dentist	298–9107
Your bank manager	770–5323
Your doctor	321–3989
Your local grocer	455–8801

Mrs. Greenfield

Mr. Sirl

Miss Brainne

Mr. Hawkins

Miss Boulton

Mrs. Woolridge

Mr. Hall (75)

Miss Finch (28)

Mrs. Knight (35)

Mr. Potter (40)

Mr. Bell (30)

Mr. Shelby (19)

Your local chemist	833–9939
Your tennis partner	539–4112
Your plumber	211–8519
Your local pub	939–1427
Your garage	147–9340

Score: ....

CARD TEST

This next test is designed to exercise your present capacity in the remembering of cards and their sequence. The list below contains all 52 cards of the regular pack in numbered order. Your task is to spend not more than 5 minutes looking at this list and then recall it in order. Give yourself one point for each correct answer, scoring yourself in the same way as you did in the Link test.

1.	King of diamonds	27.	Nine of clubs
2.	Seven of hearts	28.	Jack of diamonds
3.	Five of spades	29.	Queen of hearts
4.	Four of clubs	30.	Four of spades
5.	Three of diamonds	31.	Six of clubs
6.	Ten of hearts	32.	King of spades
7.	Queen of clubs	33.	Ace of clubs
8.	Eight of clubs	34.	Six of hearts
9.	Five of hearts	35.	Five of clubs
10.	Jack of clubs	36.	Three of hearts
11.	Ace of spades	37.	Ten of diamonds
12.	Five of diamonds	38.	Two of clubs
13.	Nine of diamonds	39.	Seven of diamonds
14.	Eight of hearts	40.	Ten of spades
15.	Ace of diamonds	41.	Three of clubs
16.	Seven of spades	42.	Eight of spades
17.	Nine of hearts	43.	King of hearts
18.	Ten of clubs	44.	Nine of spades
19.	Six of diamonds	45.	Queen of diamonds
20.	Queen of spades	46.	Ace of hearts
21.	Eight of diamonds	47.	Three of spades
22.	Four of diamonds	48.	Two of spades
23.	Six of spades	49.	Jack of spades
24.	Two of diamonds	50.	Four of hearts
25.	King of clubs	51.	Jack of hearts
26.	Two of spades	52.	Seven of clubs

Score: ....

This next test is the last. Listed below are ten fairly important historical dates. Your task is to spend not more than a
minute and a half remembering the event and the date. Give
yourself one mark for a perfectly accurate answer and half a
mark if you come within five years.

1. 1666   Fire of London
2. 1770   Beethoven's birthday
3. 1215   Signing of Magna Carta
4. 1917   Russian Revolution
5. c.1454   First Printing Press
6. 1815   Battle of Waterloo
7. 1608   Invention of the telescope
8. 1905   Einstein's theory of Relativity
9. 1789   French Revolution
10. 1776   Declaration of American Independence

Score: ....

That ends the testing. If you have done badly then you have
done as expected and are quite average!

Within the first few chapters of this book you will have
learned how to get perfect scores in less than the time allotted,
and by the time you have completed the book *all* of these tests
will be child's play. Give yourself a day's rest (after what must
have been a fairly strenuous session!) and start your first
memory training tomorrow.

CHAPTER TWO

MEMORY SYSTEM 1

THE LINK SYSTEM

Having established what I hope was not a too disturbing picture of the way in which your memory has been limited up to now, we move on to the first method of improving its ability.

The method is known as the *Link* method, and is the most basic of all the systems—the ideas and methods that you use when applying this system will prove invaluable in mastering the more sophisticated systems.

'Link' can be considered to be the key word in memory, another word for it being 'association'. Before going into the details of the link system, I shall say something about the principle of association and its connection with the entire field of Memory.

As I mentioned in the introduction, psychologists have come to the conclusion that we remember things by joining a certain part of them with other things. For example, on returning to an old home or your old school, you may have realised that seeing a certain picture on the wall, or a certain piece of furniture, etc., made you 'suddenly remember' things that you would otherwise have entirely forgotten.

Your mind was *linking* all the ideas and memories that had been *associated* with the object at which you were looking.

This principle applies, no matter how complicated the memory situation is. Even when remembering complicated mathematical formulas or very abstract ideas, there is a link in the background which triggers the memory you want. It is this basic concept that we shall make use of throughout the book, using methods that enable the mind to link or associate far more readily than it would otherwise have been able to.

Without further ado let us apply the link method of remembering to a simple shopping list. In a rushed moment, and with no paper or writing instruments nearby, you have been asked to buy the following items:

1. Bananas
2. Soap
3. Eggs
4. Drinking glasses
5. Bandages
6. Matches
7. Washing up liquid
8. Toothpaste
9. Shoes
10. Tomatoes

Most people when given a list quickly like this manage to remember six or seven of the items. If you haven't already spent some time trying to remember the list, close your eyes now *without looking at the list again*, and see how many you can recall, giving yourself extra credit if you remember the correct order.

The link method makes it all so much easier. Instead of frantically trying to remember everything randomly, you must quickly and decisively *link* the objects with each other.

In the list that we have set out to learn this can be done as follows: Bananas and Soap are both items commonly used in jokes about people falling on their behinds! Immediately imagine yourself therefore stepping on a banana peel with your right foot and a bar of soap with your left foot, causing you to fall down.

What happens when someone falls down?—He breaks things! Rather than making our memory device into a medical catalogue, we remember the next two items on our list by picturing eggs in our right hand and glasses in our left hand, both of which get broken during the fall.

Our first four items are now firmly linked together. How do we link the rest? Again the task is quite easy; bandages are used for cuts which are caused by broken glass.

Our next item, matches, can be linked with the idea of a bandage if we think of one of those long rolled bandages, the end of which has been set alight and is slowly burning. Matches!

Having created a mental fire we had better put it out. And what better device than a fire extinguisher, or a container of washing up liquid which we mentally 'put' in the fire extinguisher's place.

The next item on our list, toothpaste, can easily be linked with the washing up liquid as they both come from containers which have to be squeezed. Simply imagine a fire-extinguisher-soap-container beginning to squirt toothpaste instead of soap.

We can move rapidly onto the next item by picturing the toothpaste no longer being squirted at the fire, but being badly aimed and covering our freshly polished shoes which were about to step on a rotten tomato anyway!

And there we have it: our list of ten items neatly associated: we slip on the bananas and soap, break the eggs and drinking glasses, and need bandages which are set alight by matches. The resulting fire is then put out by washing up liquid which is similar to squeezing toothpaste which goes all over our clean shoes which were about to squash a tomato!

The system is easy, but you might have already thought 'Ah yes, it might work for *that* list, but what happens when I have to memorise my own?'.

In fact it will be just as easy for you to make up your own, and eventually even *easier*, if you follow these simple rules:

1. *Exaggerate* your associations
2. *Move* your associations.
3. *Substitute* your associations.
4. Be *Absurd!*

1. *Exaggerate Your Associations*

Items are remembered far more easily if they are pictured in your mind's eye as being much greater than they really are. For example when you pictured yourself slipping on the banana peel and the bar of soap, your remembering task would have been made easier if you imagined a banana peel the size of a ski, and a bar of soap as large as a boulder.

2. *Move Your Associations*

Whenever you are establishing links include if possible, movement or action. By doing this you create images which are far more alive. The movement in your image helps to nudge the picture back into consciousness. Imagine for example how much more difficult our shopping list would have been to memorise if we had not used the idea of falling, breaking, bleeding, burning, squirting, and squashing! Action and movement *always* make remembering not only easier, but also more enjoyable.

3. Substitute Your Associations

The art of remembering well relies on a number of factors, and it is advisable, especially in associations which you might feel are a little weak, to bring all your weapons to the fore. By substituting one thing for another you can often very strongly reinforce a link that might have been not quite strong enough. An example of this was our substitution of the fire extinguisher for the washing-up liquid container. The substitution itself made the association and the movement links more complete, and thus more readily recalled.

4. Be Absurd!

Remembering is one area where you can really 'let yourself go'. There is no point at all in being conservative about the links you form—in fact the more conservative and retiring you are, the weaker your associations will be, and the worse your memory!

Whenever you are trying to associate *anything* with anything else, think up the most extraordinary and outrageous combination you can, and you will find it will last much longer. In day-to-day living you will find the same principle works. It is never the humdrum, mundane, ordinary events that catch one's attention; it is the exciting, new and unusual events which do so.

And even if somebody *does* mention the uninteresting or boring, doesn't he always commence his statement with 'It was the most *extraordinarily* boring . . .' or 'The most *deadly* dull . . .'? In other words it is those events which *stand out* which are remembered (even if they stand out because of their mediocrity!).

As a final note, and in a hushed breath, I feel obliged to mention that associations using some form of vulgar or sexual imagery are for many people among the strongest form. In view of this, and if a sexual image seems appropriate, do not hesitate to use it. Just be sure your imagination doesn't run away with itself!

CHAPTER THREE

MEMORY SYSTEM 2

THE NUMBER-SHAPE SYSTEM

In the last chapter we established the ground-work for all our memory systems. We learned that memory is a linking process and that it can be aided by exaggeration, by movement, by substitution, and by being absurd.

We now move on to the first of the Peg memory systems. A Peg memory system differs from the link system in that it uses a special list of items which never change, and to which the items you wish to remember are joined or linked.

A Peg system can be thought of as a clothes cabinet which contains a number of hooks for hanging clothes on. The hooks never change, but the clothes which are hung on the hooks can be infinitely varied. The first system we shall use is a fairly short one which uses the numbers from 1 to 10.

It would, of course, be possible for me to give you the system outright, but it will be far more valuable if you create most of it yourself. I shall therefore explain exactly how to construct the system, and shall then progress to its practical use.

The first Peg system, which we shall call the Number-Shape system, requires initially that you think of a noun which you are reminded of by the actual shape of the number. For example, and to make your task a little easier, the memory word that most people associate with the number 2 is swan, because the number resembles very closely the shape of a swan.

I shall list the numbers from 1-10, leaving a blank beside each number for you to pencil in the words which you think *best* approximate the shape of the other nine numbers.

These words will be your constant memory hooks, so try to make sure that they are good visual images—words to which you will be able to join other ideas without too much difficulty. Give yourself not more than five minutes to complete the list from 1-10, and even if you find some numbers impossible, don't worry, just read on.

Number	Number shape memory word
1	....
2	....
3	....
4	....
5	....
6	....
7	....
8	....
9	....
10	....

Many readers will have realised while making up their Number-Shape memory words that what they were doing was using their creative imagination, while at the same time using the basic concept of linking. In other words, you were taking two basically unconnected items, a number and an object, and associating them by substituting the idea of shape.

You will probably have come up with words similar to the following:

1　Pole, pencil, pen, straw, penis
2　Swan, duck.
3　Double-chin, breasts, mole-hills
4　Table, swastika, sail
5　Hook, pregnant woman
6　Golf club, cherry
7　Fishing line, cliff, boomerang
8　Bun, hourglass, shapely woman
9　Flag, sperm, tadpole,
10　Bat and ball, Laurel & Hardy

Now, having worked out your own memory words, and having seen some other suggestions, I want you to select the Number-Shape memory word which *for you* is the best one. When you have done this print it large and clear in the box below, and put a large X through each of the previous lists. From now on you will be interested *only* in the words you have selected, and should forget the other choices.

Number	Final number shape memory word
1	....
2	....
3	....
4	....
5	....
6	....
7	....
8	....
9	....
10	....

Now I want you to test yourself! Close your eyes and mentally run through the numbers from 1–10 in order. As you come to each number mentally link it with the final Number-Shape memory word you have selected. When you have done this run through the numbers in reverse order, again linking them with your chosen word, and finally pick out numbers randomly and as quickly as you can, linking the words to the numbers. Do this exercise now.

If you managed to do this fairly successfully, you have already accomplished a memory feat which most people would find difficult, if not impossible. And what is more you will find that these associations will be so strong it will not only be easy to remember them, it will be almost impossible to forget them!

The *use* of this system is quite simple, and involves of course the idea of linking. Suppose we have a list of ten items that we wish to remember not simply by linking, but in numerical order, reverse numerical order, and random numerical order. The simple link system introduced in Chapter 2 would help us somewhat with the numerical order, but would certainly leave us straining to rattle-off reverse order and random order! The Peg system leaves us with no such problem. Let us put it to the test.

You have been asked to remember the following list of items:

1. telephone
2. farmer
3. waterfall
4. aeroplane
5. meat
6. apple
7. teapot
8. rocks
9. bicycle
10. hatpin

To remember these items in order all that it necessary is to link them with the appropriate Number-Shape memory word. Remember that when you link them the associations should be exaggerated, should be moving where possible, and should be absurd. Give yourself not more than three minutes to compete your memorisation of these items, and then test yourself as you did when you were creating the system. That is, mentally run through the items in order, in reverse order, and random order. Start this exercise now.

As a guide to those readers who might have had a little difficulty, the following are examples of possible associations:

1. For telephone you might have imagined an enormous telephone pole being toppled, with a giant telephone either on top of it or being broken by it; or a telephone with the receiver which turned into a large pencil or pen every time the phone rang.

2. For farmer you could have pictured him being attacked by a giant swan or duck, or riding fairy-tale-style on one of these giant birds.

3. The waterfall could have been cascading down an enormous double chin, over a woman's very ample bosom, or onto molehills which were flattened by the water's force.

4. Aeroplane can be remembered by imagining it covered with swastikas, crashing into an enormous table, or being absurdly propelled by means of a giant sail.

5. Meat fits very nicely onto a large hook, or a pregnant woman can be thought of as 'meaty'!

6. If golf club was your choice for number 6 then you can imagine teeing off at an apple instead of a golf ball; or the apple might be thought of as a giant mutation on a cherry tree.

7. Your fishing line could be cast into an enormous teapot; or you might be pouring tea over a cliff instead of into a cup; or a neatly placed teapot could be imagined being knocked off the table by a boomerang.

8. Buns (as they often are!) could become rocks; the hourglass could be enormous, passing rocks instead of sand for telling the time; or a shapely women might have her shape ruined because her clothes were stuffed with rocks.

9. The bicycle could be imagined as having an enormous Union Jack on the front which obscured the rider's vision causing him to wobble all over the road; it would be imagined (substituted for) a sperm racing to conception; or it could be imagined ploughing through a swamp filled with enormous tadpoles.

10. And finally the bat of the bat and ball could be thought of as a large hatpin; or some typical Laurel and Hardy prank with a hatpin could be imagined.

The examples I have given here are of course only examples, but they are included to indicate the kind of creative thinking that is necessary to establish the most effective memory links. I am sure that many of you will have devised some excellent associations, and what is necessary now is that you practise this system, and make sure that your ten Number-Shape memory words are completely second-nature to you.

One of the best ways to make sure of this is to test yourself with members of your family or with friends. Ask them to make up a list of any ten items, and to read them to you with about a five-second pause between each item. The second they have spoken the word make your association, consolidating it before they reach the next one.

You (and they!) will be amazed at the ease with which you can remember the items, and it is most impressive when you are able to repeat them in reverse and random order.

Do not worry about getting previous lists of items confused with new ones. As I mentioned before this little Peg system can be compared to coat hooks—you simply remove one association and replace it with another.

In the next chapter I shall be introducing another small system similar to this one. The two can then be combined to enable you to remember, just as easily as you have remembered ten items, twenty items. Later on in the book more sophisticated systems will be introduced which can be used for storing information you wish to remember for a long period of time. The present systems are for more immediate purposes.

Give yourself about a day to become skilled with the techniques you have learned so far and then move on to the next chapter.

CHAPTER FOUR

MEMORY SYSTEM 3

THE NUMBER-SOUND SYSTEM

Now that you have learned about the history of memory, about
the ideas of association, about the Link system, and the first
small Peg system, you are ready to progress to the next small
Peg system and to a few slightly more sophisticated Peg
systems.

Because of the knowledge you are building up as you go
along these systems will be introduced without too much
preliminary explanation as the principles already discussed are
common to all of them.

The Number-Sound system is almost identical to the
Number-Shape system except that (and this you may have
already guessed.) we think of nouns or noun-verbs which are
similar in *sound* to the number.

As in Chapter 3 I am going to list the numbers from 1–10,
leaving a blank beside each number for you to pencil in the
rhyming images which you think are best for each number.
Make sure that the images will be good memory hooks for you.

As an aid, the word which nearly everyone uses for number
5 is 'hive', the images being associated with this varying from
one enormous bumble bee leaving the hive to a sky-covering
swarm of monster bees!

As practice in linking and creative thinking has probably
already improved your mental capacity give yourself not five
minutes as previously, but three minutes to fill in the Number-
Sound memory word list from 1–10.

Number	Number sound memory word
1.	....
2.	....
3.	....
4.	....
5.	....

6. ....
7. ....
8. ....
9. ....
10. ....

As before I am going to offer you now a few alternative suggestions which I would like you to consider, and then compare and contrast them with your own choices. Having done this select the Number-Sound memory word which you consider to be best and print it in the box as you did in the previous chapter.

First then, some possible choices:

1. Sun, bun, Nun, GUN
2. Shoe, pew, loo
3. Tree, flea, knee
4. Door, moor, war
5. Hive, drive, jive
6. Sticks, wicks, pricks
7. Heaven, Devon
8. Gate, bait, weight
9. Vine, line, twine
10. Hen, den, wren

Now select the most appropriate word and enter it in the box.

Number	Number sound memory word
1.	....
2.	....
3.	....
4.	....
5.	....
6.	....
7.	....
8.	....
9.	....
10.	....

As in the last chapter, I now want you to test yourself with your chosen Number-Sound word. Close your eyes and mentally run through the numbers in order, linking each number mentally with the Number-Sound memory word you have selected. Next run through the numbers in reverse order again linking them with your chosen word, and finally pick numbers randomly and as quickly as you can, linking as you go. Spend about five minutes on this exercise now.

This list can be used in exactly the same way as the Number-Shape list, although many of you will have already realised that in a way you already possess the ability to remember *20* objects in and out of sequence.

All you have to do is to establish one of these two Peg systems as the numbers from 1–10, letting the other represent the numbers from 11–20.

Let us put this to the test. You will remember (I hope!) that Chapter 1 contained two tests, each of which asked you to remember 20 items. The first of these tests could have been adequately done by using the Link system, but the second was more difficult and required some form of Peg memory system. Let us then apply our present knowledge to the more difficult of these two tests.

Decide which of the two Peg systems is to be first, and which second and then give yourself not more than four minutes to remember the list. When your four minutes are up, close or cover the book and then write down your answers in the same way as you did in the original test. After you have done this check your answers against the list. Here it is again:

1. Tar
2. Aeroplane
3. Leaf
4. Shell
5. Hair
6. Moon
7. Lever
8. Lighter
9. Railway
10. Field
11. Atom
12. Wheel
13. School

14. Sand
15. Doctor
16. Spectacles
17. Lake
18. Feather
19. Sock
20. Pump

Score: Number correct ....

You will almost certainly have made an improvement over your performance in the original test, but might find that you are still having difficulty with certain associations. The only way to overcome this is to practise and practise still more. Tonight and tomorrow throw yourself in at the deep end, testing yourself whenever possible, and having as many of your friends and acquaintances as you can try to catch you out on lists that they make up for you to remember.

On the first few tries you will probably make a few errors but even so, you will be performing far beyond the average person's capacity. If you persevere, you will soon be able to fire back lists without any hesitation, and without any fear of making mistakes!

CHAPTER FIVE

MEMORY SYSTEM 4

THE CLASSICAL ROOM SYSTEM

Before moving on to two of the more major Peg systems, you shall have a light and easy day's work with a simple little Room system.

In the section dealing with the history of memory, I mentioned that the Romans accepted without question the theoretical ideas of memory introduced by the Greeks. I added that one of their major contributions was the introduction and development of memory systems.

One of their most popular systems made use of objects in a room. Such a system is easily constructed. Try to imagine an enormous room with a door. Now fill this room with as many items of furniture and other objects as you wish—each item of furniture will serve as a link word. Don't make a mental rubbish-dump of it, though! Your objects should be very precisely ordered.

For example, you may decide to start on the immediate right of the door as you enter the room, placing there a finely carved coffee-table, on which you might put anything from a statue to an attractive lamp. Next to this you could have an antique sofa, and so on.

You can see that the possibilities are almost limitless—but make sure that your objects are memorisable and that you can keep them mentally placed in the right order.

How is such a system used? When you are given a list of objects you wish to remember in order (it being not necessary to remember reverse, random, or numerical order), you simply associate the items to be remembered with the objects in your room. Suppose, for instance, that your first three items were 'oil', 'insect', and 'girl'. Using the examples given, the oil could be imagined flowing all over the coffee table, the insect could be enlarged and perched on top of the statue or could be flying around the lamp, and the girl could be draped seductively on the sofa!

The advantage of this system is that it is entirely your own, that the room may be as large as you wish, may have as many walls as you care to imagine, and may contain a great number of memory-peg objects.

On the blank page provided here you should now construct your own room, selecting the shape you feel is best, and then finally printing in the objects with which you are going to furnish it.

When you have completed this task, take a number of mental walks around the room until you are completely familiar with the order and arrangement of things. As with the previous memory systems, practise alone and with friends, until your system is firmly established.

In the next chapter I shall be introducing the Alphabet system, which will enable you to remember more than 20 items.

CHAPTER SIX

MEMORY SYSTEM 5

THE ALPHABET SYSTEM

The Alphabet system is another Peg system similar in construction to the Number-Shape and Number-Sound systems; but instead of using numbers, it uses the 26 letters of the alphabet.

Its advantage is that it enables you to remember 26 objects, its only disadvantage being that most people find it hard to reel off the alphabet in reverse order, or to know immediately the number order of a given letter in the alphabet.

As with the two number systems, I suggest you first construct your own list, then compare it with alternative suggestions, and finally select your own list to be entered in the memory box.

The method of constructing your Alphabet memory system is as follows: Select a word that starts with the actual sound of the letter, is visually outstanding, and comes first in the dictionary.

For example, for the letter 'L' it would be possible to use elastic, elegy, elephant, elbow, and elm, etc. If you were looking up these words in the dictionary, the first one you would come to would be elastic, and that is therefore the word you would choose.

The reason for this rule is that if you should ever forget your alphabet word, you can mentally flick through the letters in order, rapidly arriving at the correct word. In the example given, if you had forgotten your word, you would try el'a' and would immediately be able to recall your first word—elastic!

Another rule in the construction of the Alphabet memory system is that if the letter itself makes a word (for example 'I' makes 'eye') then that word should be used. In some cases it is possible to use meaningful initials instead of complete words, for example D.D.T.

I have listed the letters of the alphabet. Paying close attention to the rules for constructing the system, pencil in your own Alphabet system words.

Letter	Alphabet memory word
A	....
B	....
C	....
D	....
E	....
F	....
G	....
H	....
I	....
J	....
K	....
L	....
M	....
N	....
O	....
P	....
Q	....
R	....
S	....
T	....
U	....
V	....
W	....
X	....
Y	....
Z	....

I hope that wasn't too tiring! Many people have difficulty in constructing an Alphabet memory system, because they tend to be far more visual- than sound-oriented.

Before considering the alternative suggestions, therefore, it might be wise to re-check your own Alphabet memory words, making sure you have started your words with the *sound* of the letter or letter word and not simply the letter itself. For example 'ant', 'bottle', 'case', 'dog', and 'eddy' would not be correct memory words because they do not start with the *sound* of the letter as it is pronounced in the alphabet.

Having re-checked your own words, now compare them with the following list of suggestions, and when you have done so select your final list and print it clearly in the Alphabet memory system box. As before cross out your own list and the list of suggestions when you have finished with them.

A   Ace,—those of you with knowledge of American history might use Abe.

B   Bee—the letter makes a word; this is the word that should be used.

C   See—the same rule applies.

D   Deed (legal)—the initials D.D.T. may be preferable.

E   Easel

F   Effigy

G   Jeep, or gee-gee!

H   H-bomb

I   Eye

J   Jay—a gaily coloured member of the crow family.

K   Cage

L   Elastic, or elbow if you pronounce elastic with a long 'e'.

M   Ember

N   Enamel

O   Oboe

P   Pea—first alphabetically!

Q   Queue

R   Arch

S   Eskimo

T   Tea—or perhaps T-square.

U   U-boat—'you' is too vague

V   Vehicle, or the initials V.D.

W   Wolf—the sound here is difficult; the initials W.C. can be used instead.

X   X-ray

Y   Wife

Z   Zebra, or Z-car!

Now make your final choices and enter them in the memory box.

Letter	Final Alphabet memory word
A	....
B	....
C	....
D	....
E	....
F	....
G	....
H	....
I	....
J	....
K	....
L	....
M	....
N	....
O	....
P	....
Q	....
R	....
S	....
T	....
U	....
V	....
W	....
X	....
Y	....
Z	....

Your practice with the Alphabet system should be similar to your practice with previous smaller systems.

The end of this chapter marks the end of your learning the introductory and basic Peg and Link systems. From now on, apart from a brief summary of these concepts in Chapter 7, you will be learning more sophisticated and more expansive systems that will enable you to remember lists of *hundreds* of items, as well as systems to help you remember faces, numbers etc.

The next chapter but one deals with an exciting new system which has never been published or widely used, although it has been carefully tested.

CHAPTER SEVEN

SMALL MEMORY SYSTEM REVIEW
AND EXTENSION

You have now completed the five smaller memory systems:
the Link, the Number-Shape, the Number-Sound, the
Classical Room and the Alphabet.

Each of these systems can be used either independently or in
conjunction with another system. Furthermore, one or two of
the systems can be set aside, if you wish, as 'constant memory
banks'. That is, if you have certain lists or orders of items that
you will need to be able to recall over a period of a year or more,
you can set aside the system of your choice for this purpose.

Before moving on to the broader systems, however, I want
to introduce you to a simple and intriguing method for
instantly doubling any of the systems you have so far learned!

When you have reached the end of a system but still wish
to add further associations, all you have to do is to go back to
the beginning of your system and imagine your association
word exactly as you usually imagine it, with the exception that
it is contained *in a huge block of ice*. This simple device will
drastically change the association pictures you have formed,
and will double the effectiveness of your system by giving you
the original list plus the original list in its new context.

For example, if your first key in the Number-Shape system
was 'telephone pole', you would imagine that same telephone
pole either buried in the heart of your giant block, or protruding from the corners or sides; if your first word in the Number-
Sound system was 'sun', then you could imagine its fierce rays
melting the edges of the ice block in which it was contained;
if your first word in the Alphabet system was ace then you
could imagine a giant playing card either frozen in the centre
or forming one of the six sides of the ice cube.

Practise this technique. You will find it extraordinarily
helpful.

CHAPTER EIGHT

MEMORY SYSTEM 6

SKIPNUM

Skipnum (Self-Coding Instant Phonetic Number Memory grid.) is an entirely new memory system. It was developed by my close friend and associate Heinz Norden, the well-known writer, translator and polymath.

Skipnum differs from other major memory systems in that it is based almost entirely on phonetics. The system is based on two elements everyone knows:

1. The initial letter of the memory word is the same as the initial letter of the number which is attached to that word. For example the *numbers* from 60 to 69 all begin with an 's', and therefore so do the *memory words* for the numbers from 60 to 69.

2. The vowel sound of the memory word is the same as the vowel sound of the unit digit in the number for which we are making the word. For example let us take the number 42. The first letter in our memory word must be an 'f' because 42 begins with an 'f'. The next sound in our memory word must be 'oo' because the digit number in 42 is two, and its vowel sound is 'oo'. That means we have 'foo' which we can easily make into a word by adding either 'l' or 'd' giving us 'fool' or 'food'.

Let us try another example. The number we wish to create a memory word for is 91. The first letter is 'n'. The digit number in 91 is 1, and its vowel sound is 'uh'. To complete our memory word for 91 we simply have to complete 'nuh'. A 't' or an 'n' completes this most satisfactorily giving us 'nut' or 'nun'.

There are a few exceptions to these two basic rules, but they are logical and easily remembered.

1. *Ten to nineteen.* These numbers do not of course have the same initial consonant. They are however collectively the 'tens' or 'teens' and therefore we use the letter 't' for these numbers.

2. *Twenty to twenty-nine.* A full set of memory words

beginning with 'tw' is not available so 'tr' is used instead. We can remember this fairly easily by recalling that children often confuse 'tr' and 'tw'.

3. *Fifty to fifty-nine*. We cannot use 'f' as the initial letter because we have already used it for forty. Instead we use 'h' because it stands for 'half', and fifty is halfway between o and 100.

4. *Seventy to seventy-nine*. In the same way that we could not use 'f' for fifty because we had already used it for forty, we cannot use 's' for seventy because we have already used it for sixty. This is overcome easily by using the second consonant of seventy, i.e. 'v'.

5. *Eighty to eighty-nine*. There is no initial consonant here so instead we use the first consonant in the word eighty, which is 'g'.

6. *Vowel sound for nine*. We cannot use the 'i' sound for nine because we have already used it for five. Instead we use one of the most common remaining vowel sounds (which is contained in the word vowel.) 'ow'.

7. oo–o9. These are included in the Skipnum grid for convenience, because these two-digit units occur frequently in telephone numbers and elsewhere. We use the initial consonant 'b' because it is easy to remember when we think of oo7, James *Bond*!

Before reading on, have a quick look at the memory grid in this Chapter, trying to familiarise yourself with the ideas that have so far been explained. The grid is laid out simply and clearly, and should not be hard to follow.

You have noticed from looking at the grid that a preferred memory word is given in bold. It is usually the simplest possible word formed by the above two rules, and is preferably one that can be used both as a verb and a noun. If possible it should have more than one meaning, and should be able to serve as a connector in making phrases from the memory words. Vulgar, action and emotionally charged words are also preferable because they are easier to remember.

Where they arise, silent initial letters such as 'g' 'k' 'w' and 'y' are ignored in the memory words.

Since more than one word can often be formed within the boundaries of the rule, alternate words may be used. Some of these are given in the Skipnum grid for you to choose from. This possibility of alternate words is particularly useful in

54

SKIPNUM

SKIPNUM	Initial Consonant →	B (James Bond 007)	None	T (Teen)	TR (=baby talk TW, Twenty)	TH (Dirty)	F (Forty)	H (Halfway, 0 -100, Fifty)	S (Sixty)	V (Seventy)	G (Eighty)	N (Ninety)
Key Vowel	Decile / Last Digit	00-09	0-9	10-19	20-29	30-39	40-49	50-59	60-69	70-79	80-89	90-99
P (oh)	0	00 BOAT (BEAU BONE)	0 OWN (OWE OAF)	10 TOAST (TOLL TONE)	20 TROJAN (TROPHY TROLL)	30 THOSE (THOUGH)	40 PHONE (FOLK FOAM)	50 HOLE (HOME HOST)	60 SOAP (SOUL SO)	70 VOLE (VOTE)	80 GOAT (GOAL GO)	90 NO (NOSE NOTE)
U (wun)	1	01 BUG (BUST BUT)	1 UP (OTHER UTTER)	11 TONGUE (TON TUT)	21 TRUST (TRUCK TROUBLE)	31 THUMB (THUS THUNDER)	41 FUCK (FUN FUNK)	51 HUNT (HUT HUM)	61 SUCK (SOME SON)	71 VULGAR (VULTURE)	81 GUN (GUM GUT)	91 NUT (NOTHING NUMBER)
OO (too)	2	02 BOOT (BEAUTY BOOZE)	2 OOZE (YOOHOO YOU)	12 TOMB (TOOL TOO)	22 TROOP (TRUE)	32 THROUGH	42 FOOL (FOOD FUME)	52 WHO (HOOP)	62 SUIT (SOON SOOT)	72 VIEW (VOODOO)	82 GURU (GOOD GOON)	92 NOOSE (NOON NEW)
EE (three)	3	03 BEETLE (BEEF BEAN)	3 EAT (EAR EEL)	13 TEA (TEAM TEASE)	23 TREE (TREAT TREACLE)	33 THEATRE (THEE THESE)	43 FEET (FEEL FEAR)	53 HEAT (HE HEAL)	63 SEAL (SEE SCENE)	73 VEAL (VENAL VEER)	83 GEAR (GEEZER)	93 KNEE (NEAR NEEDLE)
O (for)	4	04 BORE (BOARD BOUGHT)	4 ALL (ORGY AWFUL)	14 TALK (TOP TORN)	24 TROT (TRAWL TROMBONE)	34 THORN (THAW THOUGHT)	44 FALL (FOR FOUGHT)	54 WHORE (HORN HALL)	64 SORE (SAUCER SAW)	74 VAULT (VAUNT VON)	84 GONE (GORMLESS GALL)	94 KNOT (KNOB GNAW)
EYE (five)	5	05 BY (BUY) (BIKE BIND)	5 EYE (I ICE)	15 TIE (TIME TIGHT)	25 TRY (TRIAL TRIPLE)	35 THIGH (THY THYME)	45 FIRE (FIGHT FINE)	55 HIGH (HIDE HIKE)	65 SIGN (SIGHT SIBERIA)	75 VIPER (VILE VICE)	85 GUY (GUIDE GUILE)	95 NIGHT (KNIFE NICE)
I (six)	6	06 BIG (BIT BILL)	6 IT (IF ILL)	16 TIT (TIP TILL)	26 TRICK (TRIPLE TRIM)	36 THIN (THIS THINK)	46 FIX (FIT FILL)	56 HIT (HILL HIM)	66 SICK (SIT SING)	76 VICAR (VIGOUR VILLAGE)	86 GIMMICK (GIZZARD)	96 NIT (NIL NIP)
E (seven)	7	07 BED (BELL BEST)	7 EGG (END ETC)	17 TELL (TEND TEMPO)	27 TREMBLE (TREAD TREND)	37 THEM (THEN THREAT)	47 FELT (FENDER FED)	57 HELL (HELP HEMP)	67 SET (SELL SEND)	77 VELVET (VET VENEER)	87 GHETTO (GUEST GET)	97 NEST (NET NEVER)
A (ate)	8	08 BAY (BABY BAIT)	8 ACHE (ATE AIM)	18 TAPE (TAIL TAME)	28 TRAIN (TRAY TRAITOR)	38 THEY	48 FAKE (FATE FAIL)	58 HAY (HATE HAIL)	68 SALE (SAME SAY)	78 VEIL (VAPOUR)	88 GAY (GAME GAIN)	98 NEIGHBOUR (NAIL NAME)
OW (how, our)	9	09 BOWEL (BOUND BOUT)	9 OWL (OUT HOUR)	19 TOWN (TOWEL TOWER)	29 TROUT (TROWEL)	39 THOU	49 FOUND (FOUL FOWL)	59 HOW (HOWL HOUND)	69 SOUND (SOUR SAUDI)	79 VOW (VOWEL)	89 GOUT (GOWN)	99 NOW (NOUN NOWT)

55

situations where you might be trying to remember a long number which contains the same two-digit sequence more than once. You don't have to repeat the same word, but can use another word representing the same number!

Another advantage of this memory system is that you don't have to learn the memory words by heart since they are 'self coding'. They will pop into your mind instantly as long as you know the rules.

Up to this point in the Chapter you have been given a lot of detailed information which at the moment you may have found a little bit difficult to absorb completely. It is advisable now to review quickly the entire Chapter, consolidating those areas which have given you some trouble. To assist you in further consolidation, I have randomly listed the numbers from 1–100 on the next two pages so that you can readily test yourself in either remembering the words on the grid or 'self coding' your own.

When you have completed the Skipnum grid to your satisfaction take the plunge and try to remember 100 items. You will find to your surprise that it is not really much more difficult than remembering twenty! When you are confident test yourself with your friends.

58. ....
49. ....
05. ....
5. ....
52. ....
31. ....
93. ....
54. ....
99. ....
8. ....
13. ....
63. ....
38. ....
03. ....
79. ....
92. ....
41. ....
0. ....
37. ....
29. ....
00. ....
73 ....
56. ....
97. ....
68. ....
9. ....
22. ....
51. ....

60. ....
39. ....
2. ....
48. ....
69. ....
84. ....
70. ....
4 ....
15. ....
57. ....
01. ....
94. ....
88. ....
34. ....
18. ....
85. ....
87. ....
30. ....
59. ....
89. ....
74. ....
27. ....
50. ....
86. ....
67. ....
65. ....
61. ....
90. ....

35.	10. ....
44.	83. ....
47.	21. ....
07.	36. ....
96.	08. ....
77.	7. ....
20.	32. ....
12.	75. ....
16.	78. ....
62.	26. ....
80.	40. ....
71.	3. ....
02.	43. ....
14.	76. ....
6.	09. ....
19.	72. ....
98.	33. ....
66.	46. ....
53.	23. ....
82.	28 ....
1.	95. ....
25.	81. ....
04.	06. ....
17.	11. ....
64.	42. ....
45.	24. ....
55.	91. ....

CHAPTER NINE

MEMORY SYSTEM FOR NAMES AND FACES

Remembering names and faces is one of the most important aspects in our lives, and one of the most difficult.

In every walk of life, every level of occupation, and every social situation, there are literally millions of people who say they 'just can't remember' the people they meet.

In business and the professions this can be most embarrassing. If you are at a conference, attending a course, or involved in any situation in which you are meeting new people, it is not only *embarrassing* to be unable to remember the names and faces of those who are with you, it can also be a serious handicap when you meet them again. Even should you not have occasion to meet them again, the ability to remember names and faces without seeing them may be useful when you are 'mentally thumbing through' people who might be of assistance to you.

In a social setting, the inability to remember the names and faces of people you meet is a discomforting and unpleasant experience. Many people devise little tricks and methods for evading the issue.

One of the favourites is to ask for the person's name, and when he replies with his Christian name to say 'Oh, I knew that! it was your *surname* I had difficulty remembering', and of course if he replies with his surname 'Oh I knew *that*! it was your *Christian* name I had difficulty remembering'! The disadvantages of this little technique are two-fold: Even if it works you have had to admit that at least *in part* you had forgotten his name; and secondly, many people reply immediately with both their Christian *and* surnames!

Another device commonly used by people who have forgotten a name is to say something like 'Oh, I *am* sorry, but how was it that you spelled your name?' This of course can work in situations where a person has a name like Pattlesserie Zhytniewski! But when the retort is a sarcastic 'J-O-H-N S-M-I-T-H' you can be made to look a little silly!

These tricks *are* nothing more than tricks, and apart from the obvious pitfalls I have mentioned they inevitably leave the person who is using them in an insecure and uncomfortable position. Aware of his inadequacy, he tends to be afraid that his tricks won't work or that he will be placed in a situation where they will be inappropriate and his poor memory will be on full view! Tricks, then, are not enough.

At the other end of the scale from the person who 'just can't remember' names and faces, is that well-known person who always *does* remember. At school it might have been a particular teacher (or the *headmaster*!); at university a well-known professor, and in business a successful manager. Whatever the situation I am sure you will confirm the fact that the person was socially confident, generally successful, and almost certainly well-known.

I remember well the first class I ever attended at university. It was an eight-in-the-morning English lecture, and the excitement of the first day and the first class had not quite managed to shake off the sleepiness from most of the students.

Our professor had! He strode into the room with no brief-case and no books, stood in front of the class, announced his name, and then said he would call the attendance. He started alphabetically, listing off names such as Abrahamson, Adams, Ardlett, and Bush, in response to which he got the usual mumbled 'Yes, sir' and 'Here, sir'. When he came to Cartland, however, there was no reply. He paused for a moment and then said 'Mr. John Cartland'. To which there was still no reply. Without change of expression he then said 'Mr. John W. P. Cartland?' and proceeded to list the boy's birthday, address, and telephone number! There was still no reply so our professor (who by this time had thoroughly awakened the class!) carried on with the remaining names. Each time he arrived at the name of a person who was absent he called out that persons initials, birthday, address and telephone number!

When he had completed the roster and everyone sat with jaws hanging open, he repeated very rapidly the names of all the students who were absent and said, with a wry smile on his face, 'I'll make a note of them some time!'

He never forgot one of us, either!

From that day on he became a legend, for none of us could imagine or hope to compete with the brilliance of a mind that could so completely and perfectly remember names and dates.

We were, of course, mistaken. Using the proper memory system, the kind of performance that our professor gave is by no means an impossibility, and is in fact quite simple.

In this chapter I shall introduce you to the systems and techniques that make remembering of names, faces and related facts a relatively simple and certainly a rewarding task.

Before getting down to the specific methodology, there are a few rules that should be observed, even when one is not using special memory systems. These rules or pointers apply mostly to situations in which you are meeting new people. The pointers rely on one of the most important factors in memory:

Repetition.

When you are introduced to somebody *first* make sure you listen. Many people actually 'turn off' when they are introduced to people and haven't the faintest idea what the name of the person is to whom they have just been introduced!

Second, request that the name be repeated even if you have heard it. Most people tend to mumble introductions and even if an introduction is clear no one will be disturbed if you ask for a repetition.

Third, repeat the name when you have been given it the second time. Rather than saying simply 'how do you do?' add the name to the end of your greeting: 'how do you do, Mr. Rosenthal'.

Fourth, if the name is at all difficult, politely ask for the spelling.

Fifth, if the situation seems to warrant it ask the person something about the background and history of his name.

Contrary to what you might expect most people will be flattered by your interest, and pleased that you have taken the trouble to enquire about their name and remember it.

Carrying the principles of repetition and involvement further, make sure that during conversations with people you newly meet you repeat the name wherever possible. This repetition helps to implant the name more firmly in your memory, and is also socially more rewarding, for it involves the other person more intimately in the conversation. It is far more satisfying to hear you say 'yes, as Mr. Jones has just said . . .' than to hear you say 'yes, as this chap over here has just said . . .'!

And finally of course when you are taking leave of those you have met make sure you say, rather than just an impersonal farewell, 'good evening, Mr. Jones'.

These aids to memory are, as I mentioned, useful to the person who is not using memory systems as well as one who is, although they are naturally far more beneficial to the latter, because he has additional 'artillery' which he can use to back himself up. Without further ado, let us learn the system for remembering faces and names.

To begin with, we must become far more observant of the faces we wish to remember! Many people, especially those who have a poor memory for names and faces, have great difficulty in remembering how one face differs from another, and find it almost impossible to describe the individual characteristics of faces. Our first task then is to become more *observant*.

To aid you in this the next few pages will give you a 'guided tour' from the top of the head to the tip of the chin, enumerating the various characteristics and the ways in which they can be classified and typified. You may well be surprised at just how varied faces can be!

HEAD AND FACIAL CHARACTERISTICS

1. *The Head*

Usually you will first meet a person face-on, so before dealing with the run-down of separate characteristics we will consider the head as a whole. Look for the general shape of the entire bone structure. You will find that this can be:

    a. Large
    b. Medium
    c. Small

And that within these three categories the following shapes can be found:

    a. square
    b. rectangular
    c. round
    d. oval
    e. triangular, with the base at the chin and the point at the scalp
    f. triangular with the base and the scalp and the point at the chin

g. broad
h. narrow
i. big-boned
j. fine-boned

You may, fairly early in your meeting, see the head from the side and will be surprised at how many different shapes heads seen from this view can take:

a. square
b. rectangular
c. oval
d. broad
e. narrow
f. round
g. flat at the front
h. flat on top
i. flat at the back
j. domed at the back
k. face angled with jutting chin and slanted forehead
l. face angled with receding chin and prominent forehead

2. The Hair

In earlier days, when hairstyles used to be more consistent and lasting, hair served as a better memory hook than it does now. The advent of dyes, sprays, wigs, and almost infinitely varied styles makes identification by this feature a somewhat tricky business! Some of the more basic characteristics, however, can be listed as follows:

Men

a. thick
b. fine
c. wavy
d. straight
e. parted
f. receding
g. bald
h. cropped
i. medium
j. long
k. frizzy
l. colour (only in notable cases)

Women   a. thick
            b. thin
            c. fine

Because of the variability in women's hairstyles it is not advisable to try to remember them from this characteristic!

3. *Forehead*

Foreheads can be generally divided into the following categories:

    a. high
    b. wide
    c. narrow between hairline and eyebrows
    d. narrow between temple and temple
    e. smooth
    f. lined horizontally
    g. lined vertically

4. *Eyebrows*

    a. thick
    b. thin
    c. long
    d. short
    e. meeting at the middle
    f. spaced apart
    g. flat
    h. arched
    i. winged
    j. tapered

5. *Eyelashes*

    a. thick
    b. thin
    c. long
    d. short
    e. curled
    f. straight

6. *Eyes*

    a. large
    b. small
    c. protruding

    d. deep-seated
    e. close together
    f. spaced apart
    g. slanted outwards
    h. slanted inwards
    i. coloured
    j. iris—entire circle seen
    k. iris—circle covered partly by upper and/or
        lower lid

Attention may also be paid in some cases to the lid above and the bag below the eye, both of which can be large or small, smooth or wrinkled, and puffy or firm.

7. *The Nose*

When seen from the front:

    a. large
    b. small
    c. narrow
    d. medium
    e. wide

When seen from the side:

    a. straight
    b. flat
    c. pointed
    d. blunt
    e. snub or upturned
    f. Roman or aquiline
    g. Greek, forming straight line with forehead
    h. concave (caved in)

The base of the nose can also vary considerably in relation to the nostrils:

    a. lower
    b. level
    c. a little higher

The nostrils themselves can also vary:

    a. straight
    b. curved down
    c. flaring

    d. wide
    e. narrow
    f. hairy

8. *Cheekbones*

Cheekbones are often linked very closely with the characteristics of the face when seen front-on, but the following three characteristics may often be worth noting:

    a. high
    b. prominent
    c. obscured

9. *Ears*

Ears are a part of the face that few people pay attention to, and yet their individuality can be greater than any other feature. They may be:

    a. large
    b. small
    c. gnarled
    d. smooth
    e. round
    f. oblong
    g. triangular
    h. flat against the head
    i. protruding
    j. hairy
    k. large lobed
    l. no lobe

This feature is of course more appropriate as a memory hook with men than with women, because the latter usually cover their ears with hair.

10. *Lips*

    a. Long upper lip
    b. short upper lip
    c. small
    d. thick (bee-stung)
    e. wide
    f. thin
    g. upturned

    h. downturned
    i. Cupid's bow (U Thant)
    j. well-shaped
    k. ill-defined

11. *Chin*

When seen straight on the chin may be:

    a. long
    b. short
    c. pointed
    d. square
    e. round
    f. double (or multiple)
    g. cleft
    h. dimpled

When seen from the side it will be either:

    a. jutting
    b. straight
    c. receding

12. *Skin*

Finally the skin should be observed. It may be:

    a. smooth
    b. rough
    c. dark
    d. fair
    e. blemished or marked in some way
    f. oily
    g. dry
    h. blotchy
    i. doughy
    j. wrinkled
    k. furrowed

Other characteristics of faces, specially men's, include the various and varied growth of facial hair ranging from short sideburns to the full-blooded and face-concealing beard with moustache. There is no point in listing all the variations. It should suffice to note that these hirsute phenomena do exist, but that they, like hairstyles and colours, can change dramatically overnight.

Having acquired all this information about the face, how do we make use of it? You may be surprised to learn that the answer is contained in the earlier chapters of the book! To put it briefly all that we have to do is the following:

1. Make a definite note of the name of the person.

2. Examine his face very carefully noting the characteristics that have been enumerated in the preceding pages.

3. Look for characteristics which are unusual, extraordinary, or unique.

4. Mentally reconstruct the person's face, *exaggerating* in the way that a caricaturist does these noteworthy features.

5. *Link*, using *exaggeration* and *movement* etc, where possible, these outstanding features to the name of the person.

The best way for you to learn the application of these methods is to practise them, so following I have doubled the number of faces and names you were asked to remember in your original test, have given suggestions for linking them, and then have rearranged the faces without names for you to test your new skills.

'An impossible task!' you might say. But before you actually test yourself on these names let's look at each person separately to see what kind of associations we can make between the face and the name.

Mrs. Ruff. Mrs. Ruff has a fairly distinct hairstyle which it is unlikely that a woman such as she would change. It doesn't take much imagination to change her hair into an Elizabethan ruff—the frilled neck collar common to that age.

Mr. Hind has enormous jowls. As a matter of fact they look a little bit like a person's posterior! Be*Hind*!

Mr. Pickett. The outstanding feature of Mr. Pickett's face is it's overall rectangular quality and its straight neck. An image can conveniently be made using the type of placard that people on strike who are picketing their employers carry. To make the image more complete, you might even imagine the word 'picket' being written on the placard.

Mr. Rolls is perhaps one of the easiest. His triple chin bulging in *rolls* beneath his face makes no other image necessary.

Miss Shute. Attractive though she may be, Miss Shute has one of those characteristically in-curved noses, a little similar

Mrs. Ruff

Mr. Hind

Mr. Pickett

Mr. Rolls

Miss Shute

Mr Sawyer

Mrs. Knapp

Mr. Marshall

Mr. Callis

Miss Hammant

Mr. Dockerill

Mrs. Nash

Mr. Swallow

Mrs. Cirkell

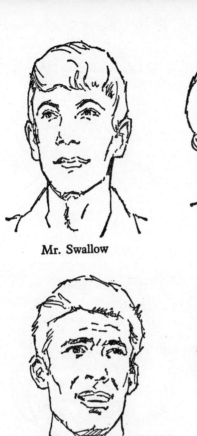

Mr. Lynch

Mrs. Paukowski

Mr. Fieldwick

Mr. Ray

Miss Sherriton   Mr. Newell

Mrs. Carstairs   Mr. Dombrower

Mrs. Heyburn   Miss Jazcolt

to a certain famous comedian. We can exaggerate this variously imagining a giant coal-chute, or a fairground shoot-the-chute.

Mr. Sawyer. The outstanding characteristic on this man's face is his large, straight and shaggy eyebrow. With a quick mental twist we convert this into a large saw, the shaggy sections of the eyebrow representing the teeth of the saw.

Mrs. Knapp. Mrs. Knapp is noticeable for the fairly large bags beneath her eyes. Concentrate on this aspect and imagine that these were caused by a lack of sleep. In other words they might go away if she were more often able to take a nap.

Mr. Marshall. Fairly obviously Mr. Marshall would be noticed for his large protruding ears. To link them with his name is not as difficult as it might appear: Imagine that each ear is a gun holster!

Mr. Callis. A number of features might be picked for Mr. Callis, but probably the best is his rough pock-marked skin. Our link here is the word 'callous', which refers to a hardened or rough area on the body's surface.

Miss Hammant. Two features should immediately strike you about Miss Hammant. First her beefy, strong face, and second her rather small nose. The caricature is easy: make the beef into a large ham; make the small nose into an ant crawling over the ham.

Mr. Dockerill. Mr Dockerill is slightly more difficult than Miss Hammant, but he is not impossible! To begin with he is a large man, which fits in with the general impression of a docker. Add to this his large eyes (like *harbours!*) and the first part of his name—Docker—is easily remembered. Further more he does look a little run down, many of his features tending to either droop or sag. We thus arrive at 'ill' and the complete Dockerill.

Mrs. Nash. One of the most noticeable characteristics of Mrs. Nash is her upper lip which is drawn back, leaving her upper front teeth slightly uncovered. To remember her name we concentrate on the teeth rather than on the lip, thinking of the *gnashing* of teeth.

Mr. Swallow. Mr. Swallow is an ideal subject! For those people to whom the word swallow immediately brings to mind images of eating or drinking he has a prominent adam's apple which can be exaggerated with ease. For those who are more inclined to ornithology his fine arched eyebrows look very much like a swallow in flight!

Mrs. Cirkell. Again an easy one! With this face we need not be concerned with particular characteristics—simply the overall shape which is circular circle—Cirkell.

Mr. Lynch. In remembering Mr. Lynch let us try a different approach. We will think first of a lynching, realising that it concentrates on the neck! Next we will link this image with our man. Mr. Lynch has a particularly *thick* neck so we imagine an especially strong rope being needed to complete the job!

Mrs. Paukowski. Of Mrs. Paukowski's major features, one of the most outstanding is her large, sloping forehead. To remember her name we convert this into an enormous ski-slope, and imagine (here we have to get really ridiculous, which is good!) a poverty striken cow skiing or attempting to ski down the slope: poor-cow-ski!

Mr. Fieldwick. Another person whose memory-feature is to be the forehead. Mr. Fieldwick's forehead is noticeable not for its size or shape, but for the wrinkles and creases upon it. Imagine it therefore as a ploughed *field*. His tufty hair can be likened to a candle-wick. A field above which there is a wick.

Mr. Ray. This young man is noticeable not so much for any particular feature, but for the general quality that emanates from his face. It seems almost to glow. A quick mental trip takes us from 'glow' to 'gleam' to 'ray'.

Miss Sheriton. Miss Sheriton is made even more attractive than she would otherwise be by the large dimple in her chin. Think of the dimple as a large cherry, so large that it weighs a ton. A slight slurring of the 'ch' gives us 'sh' Sheriton.

Mr. Newell. As with Mrs. Paukowski Mr. Newell's memory-feature is his nose, although in his case we are interested in the fact that it is slightly shiny and flared at the nostril. The shiny quality can easily be interpreted as *new*ness, and the flared nostril can be likened to a well.

Mrs. Carstairs. Rather than attempting to combine two images here we will concentrate on Mrs. Carstairs eyes which are noticeably round. The image is of a car's headlights. We need not imagine stairs, as the round eyes themselves *stare*. In other words we imagine: car stares!

Mr. Dombrower. This intelligent looking gentleman is characteristic of the 'intellectual' or 'highbrow' look because of his large, domed forehead or brow. The link is easy: dome-brow.

Mrs. Heyburn. Mrs. Heyburn has lank, straight hair. Imagine it as cut hay, and then set the lot on fire!

Miss Jazcolt. Miss Jazcolt has pouting lips which can quite easily be imagined playing an instrument such as the trumpet—jazz! She is also 'frisky' in appearance. just like a colt. Miss Jazzcolt.

That completes our list of 24 names. Before proceeding to the following pages in which you will be testing your memory of these names, quickly run back over the list and the associations, fixing them firmly in your mind.

You should by now be quite an expert at remembering names and faces. Before this chapter comes to an end, however, we shall quickly cover the memorisation of facts related to the names and faces we wish to remember.

Now that you have basically grasped the link system and the remembering of names and faces, this next step will be quite simple. All you have to do is to add another link to the face-name picture you already have.

For example, if Mrs. Ruff were a typist, you would imagine either: a typewriter within the Elizabethan ruff; typing on an Elizabethan ruff; or a typewriter sitting on Mrs. Ruff's head!

If Mr. Sawyer were a college professor you could imagine him standing in front of his class sawing his desk or lecturn in two!

If Mr. Swallow were an apprentice plumber you could imagine him swallowing his employer's tools, and so on!

One other point about remembering people is the following: if you are *certain* that you will be meeting this person only once and that you are not concerned with long-term memory, it is often useful to use an outstanding item of clothing that the person might be wearing. This method of course is no good for long-term memory, as the person may not be wearing the same clothes next time.

Another general pointer concerns names that are common, such as Smith and Jones. To remember people with names like these, establish a 'Smith-chain' and a 'Jones-chain' etc. To do this pick a 'basic Smith' or Jones and use that person's face as a link with any other person having the same name. You will find that the more people you have on the chain, the easier remembering becomes.

And finally, how *did* my professor perform his amazing feat? By now the answer should be fairly apparent: firstly he used

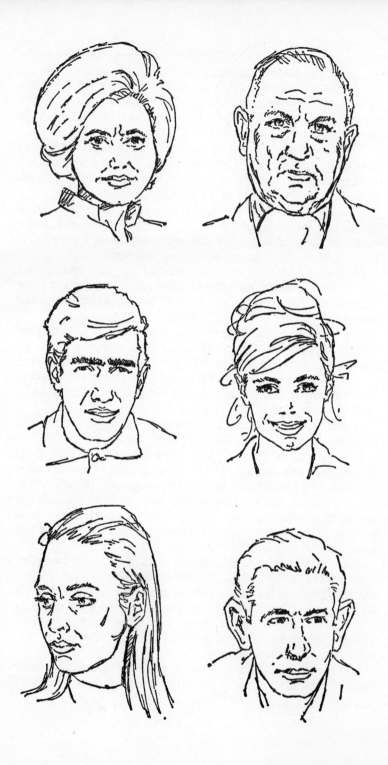

one of the basic list systems to remember the names in the proper order, obviously making extravagant associations with the memory word and the name to be remembered. The numbers and addresses he remembered by a system with which I will be dealing in a later chapter. Once he had called our names and we had identified ourselves, the rest was easy. He linked the names with the very motley collection of faces in the class.

CHAPTER TEN

THE MAJOR SYSTEM

The Major system is the ultimate in the development of the peg systems discussed earlier. It is a system which has been in use for over 400 years, although it has been continually improved since the middle of the 17th century, when it was introduced by Stanislaus Mink von Wesnnsshein. Von Wennsshein's basic construction was modified in the early 18th century by Doctor Richard Grey, an Englishman.

The system makes use of a different consonant or consonant sound for each number from zero to ten as follows:

```
1 = t, d, th
2 = n
3 = m
4 = r
5 = l
6 = j, sh, ch, dg, soft g
7 = k, ch, hard c, hard g, ng, q
8 = f, v
9 = p, b
0 = s, z, soft c
```

To save you the trouble of remembering these by rote, there are simple little remembering devices:

1. The letters t and d have *one* down stroke.
2. The letter n has *two* down strokes.
3. The letter m has *three* down strokes.
4. The letter r is the last letter in the word *four*.
5. The letter l can be thought of as either the roman numeral for 50 or the shape of a spread hand which has *five* spread fingers.
6. The letter J is the mirror image of 6.
7. The letter k, when seen as a capital, contains two number *sevens* .

8. The letter f, when written, has two loops; similar to the number 8.

9. The letter p is the mirror image of 9.

10. s or z is the first sound of the word zero; 'o' is the last letter.

As with the Number-Sound and Number-Shape systems, our task is to create a visual image that can immediately and permanently be linked with the number it represents.

Let us take for example the number 1. In order to assign to it a memory word we have to think of a word that is a good visual image and that contains only 't', 'd' or 'th' and a vowel sound. Examples include 'toe', 'doe', tea', 'the' and many others. When recalling the word we had chosen for number 1, let us say 'tea', we would *know* that it could represent only the number 1 because the consonant letters in the word represent no other number, and vowels do not count as numbers in our system.

Let us try another example: the number 34. In this case we have first the number three which is represented by the letter 'm' and then 4 which is represented by the letter 'r'. Examples can include 'more', 'moor', 'mire' and 'mare'. In selecting the 'best' word for this number you once again make use of the alphabetic dictionary-order to assist both in choice of word and in recall.

The letters we have to choose are 'm' and 'r', so we simply mentally run through the vowels 'a-e-i-o-u' order using the first vowel that enables us to make an adequate memory word. The case in question is easily solved, as 'a' fits in between 'm' and 'r' to direct us towards the word 'mare'"

The advantage of using this alphabet-order system is that should a word in the major system ever be forgotten it can literally be 'worked out' from the basic information. All you have to do is to place the letters of the number in their correct order and then 'slot in' the vowels. As soon as you touch the correct combination your memory-word will immediately come to mind.

Before going on, jot down the numbers from 10 to 19, letting the letter t represent in each case the 'l' of the number. Next try to complete the words, using the alphabet-order system for these numbers.

Don't worry if this exercise proves a little difficult, as just over the page you will find a complete list of memory words for the numbers 1 to 100. Don't simply accept them—check each one carefully, changing any that you find difficult to visualise or for which you have a better substitute.

You now possess a peg memory system for the numbers from 1 to 100—a system which contains within itself the pattern for its own memorisation! As you will have seen, this system is basically limitless. In other words, now that we have letters for the numbers 0–9, it should be possible for us to devise memory words for the numbers not only for 1 to 100 but also for the numbers from 100 to 1,000! This system could of course go on for ever but I doubt that anyone would need more than 1,000 peg words.

On the pages that follow I have devised a list of key memory peg words for the numbers 100 to 1,000. After certain of the more 'difficult' words I have included either:

1. A suggestion for a way in which an image might be formed from the word.

2. A dictionary definition of the word, the definition including words or ideas that should help you to form your image.

3. 'New' definitions for words which place them in a humourous, or different, but certainly more memorisable form.

The remaining words have blank spaces following them. In the space provided you should write in your own key words for, or ideas about, the image you will be using.

In some cases, where the combination of letters makes the use of single words impossible, double words have been used such as 'No Cash' for the number 276, (n, hard c, sh).

In other cases it is necessary to include vowels (which have no numerical meaning) at the beginning of the word. For example the number 394 (m, p, r) is represented by the word 'empire'.

In still further cases words have been used, the first three letters *only* of which pertain to the number. For example the number 359 (m, l, b) is represented by the word '*mailbag*'. The final 'g' has no significance or importance.

Your next task should be to check carefully this Major System list. It would obviously be too much to ask you to do this at one sitting, so I suggest the more modest goal of checking, making images for, and remembering, a hundred words each day. As you go through the list make *every effort* to make your images of the words as *solid* as you possibly can.

1. TEA
2. NOAH
3. MA
4. RAY
5. LAW
6. JAW
7. KEY
8. FOE
9. PA
10. TOES
11. TATE (the Art Gallery)
12. TAN
13. TAM
14. TAR
15. TAIL
16. TAJ (Mahal)
17. TACK
18. TOFFEE
19. TAP
20. NOSE
21. NET
22. NAN
23. NAME
24. NERO
25. NAIL
26. NICHE
27. NECK
28. NAVE
29. NAP
30. MACE
31. MAT
32. MAN
33. MAMA
34. MARE
35. MALE
36. MASH
37. MAC
38. MAFIA
39. MAP
40. RACE
41. RAT
42. RAIN
43. RAM
44. REAR
45. RAIL
46. RASH
47. RACK
48. RAVE
49. RAPE
50. LACE

51. LAD	76. CAGE
52. LANE	77. CAKE
53. LAMB	78. CAFE
54. LAIR	79. CAB
55. LILY	80. FACE
56. LASH	81. FAT
57. LAKE	82. FAN
58. LAUGH	83. FOAM
59. LAP	84. FAIR
60. CHASE	85. FALL
61. CHAT	86. FISH
62. CHAIN	87. FAKE
63. CHIME	88. FIFE
64. CHAIR	89. FOB
65. CHILL	90. BASE
66. JUDGE	91. BAT
67. CHECK	92. BAN
68. CHAFF	93. BEAM
69. CHAP	94. BAR
70. CASE	95. BALL
71. CAT	96. BASH
72. CAN	97. BACK
73. CAM (Shaft)	98. BEEF
74. CAR	99. BABE
75. CALL	100. DISEASE

Even when words refer to ideas or concepts, bring them down to a more immediately imaginistic level. For example the number 368, represented by the memory words 'much force' should not be pictured as some vague power or energy in space, but should be solidified into an image in which much force is used to accomplish or destroy, etc. In other words in each of these cases you will be attempting to make the memory word as *visual* and as *memorable* as possible. Remember the four rules in the early chapter: Exaggerate; Move; Substitute; be Absurd.

In cases where words are similar in concept to previous words, it is most important to make your images as different as possible. The same caution applies to words which are pluralised because of the addition of 's'. In these cases imagine an *enormous* number of the items as opposed to a single enormous item.

You will find your consolidation of the words in the major system useful not only because it will enable you to remember the astounding number of 1,000 items in order or randomly, but also because it will exercise your creative linking ability which is so necessary for remembering *anything*.

In addition, a number of the words used as nmemonics in this Major System are interesting in their own right. As you check through and memorise each list of 100, have a dictionary by your side—it will serve as a means of solidifying the images for you, will enable you to select the best possible images or words and will be of value in the *improvement of your general vocabulary*. If you are also reading my book *Speed Reading*, combine where feasible the vocabulary exercises included in it with your exercises on the Major System.

100.	Disease.
101.	Dust.
102.	Design.
103.	Dismay.
104.	Desert.
105.	Dazzle.
106.	Discharge.
107.	Disc.

108. Deceive.	
109. Despair.	
110. Dates.	Succulent, sticky fruit, often eaten at Christmas.
111. Deadwood.	Decayed, often twisted remains of trees.
112. Deaden.	
113. Diadem.	A crown; a wreath of leaves or flowers worn around the head.
114. Daughter.	
115. Detail.	
116. Detach.	
117. Toothache.	
118. Dative.	Nouns which express giving.
119. Deathbed.	
120. Tennis.	
121. Dent.	
122. Denun.	To take a nun or nuns away from a place or situation.
123. Denim.	A very tough fabric used for making working clothes.
124. Dinner.	
125. Downhill.	
126. Danish.	A native of Denmark; like the Great Dane dog.
127. Dank.	Unpleasantly soaked or damp; marshy or swampy.
128. Downfall.	
129. Danube.	The river (or picture waltzing to the Blue Danube).
130. Demise.	The death of a sovereign.
131. Domed.	Having a large, rounded summit, as a head or a church.

87

132. Demon.

133. Demi-monde. The fringe of Society.

134. Demure.

135. Dimly.

136. Damage.

137. Democracy.

138. Dam full.

139. Damp.

140. Dress. (It may be helpful here to imagine the garment on a man.)

141. Dart.

142. Drain.

143. Dram.

144. Drawer.

145. Drill.

146. Dredge. Apparatus for bringing up mud (or oysters) from the sea or river bottom.

147. Drag.

148. Drive.

149. Drip.

150. Deluxe.

151. Daylight.

152. Delinquent.

153. Dilemma. A position leaving a choice which is usually between two evils.

154. Dealer.

155. Delilah. Temptress; false and wily woman (Samson).

156. Deluge. A great flood; Noah's flood.

157.	Delicacy.	
158.	Delphi.	The Greek town in which was the sanctuary of the oracle.
159.	Tulip.	
160.	Duchess.	
161.	Dashed.	
162.	Dudgeon.	Strong anger, resentment or feeling of offence.
163.	Dutchman.	
164.	Dodger.	A wily, tricky, elusive person.
165.	Dash light.	(Imagine the dash light in your car.)
166.	Dishwash.	Abbreviation for dishwashing machine.
167.	De choke.	(Reverse the image of choke, either in relation to a car or to strangling someone!)
168.	Dishevel.	To make the hair or clothes loose, dis-ordered, 'flung about'.
169.	Dish-up.	To serve food—usually applied to a slap-dash manner.
170.	Decks.	
171.	Decade.	
172.	Token.	
173.	Decamp.	(Imagine confusion in the dismantling of tents, etc.)
174.	Decree.	An order made by an authority demanding some kind of action.
175.	Ducal.	(Imagine anything similar to or looking like a Duke.)
176.	Duckish.	
177.	Decaying.	
178.	Take-off.	

179. Decapitate.

180. Deface.

181. Defeat.

182. Divan.

183. Defame. To speak evil of; to slander.

184. Diver.

185. Defile.

186. Devotion.

187. Defeat.

188. Two Frisky Fillies. (Imagine them in a field or memorable enclosure.)

189. Two Frightened Boys. (Perhaps being chased by 188!)

190. Debase. To lower in character, quality, or value.

191. Debate.

192. Debone. To pick the bones out of—usually from fish.

193. Whitebeam. A tree with long, silvery underleaves.

194. Dipper. (Imagine the Big Dipper star constellation.)

195. Dabble.

196. Debauch. To corrupt or lead astray from temperance or chastity.

197. Dipping. (Imagine someone being dipped forcibly into water, as the medieval torture.)

198. Dab off. (Imagine a stain or blood being 'dabbed off' with cotton wool.)

199. Depip. To take the pips out of (imagine a pomegranate!).

200. Nieces.

201. Nosed.	Sniffed or smelled out—often applied to hunting animals.
202. Insane.	
203. Noisome.	Harmful, noxious, ill-smelling.
204. Noser.	A very strong headwind.
205. Nestle.	
206. Incision.	A clean cutting of something, as with a doctor's scalpel.
207. Nosegay.	A bunch of sweet-scented flowers.
208. Unsafe.	
209. Newsboy.	
210. Notice.	
211. Needed.	
212. Indian.	
213. Anatomy.	
214. Nadir.	The lowest point; place or time of great depression.
215. Needle.	
216. Night-watch.	
217. Antique.	
218. Native.	
219. Nit-boy.	A boy who is always doing addle-headed things.
220. Ninnies.	A group of people with weak minds; Simpletons.
221. Ninth.	(Imagine the ninth hole of a golf course.)
222. Ninon.	A light-weight dress fabric made of silk.
223. Noname.	(Imagine a person who has forgotten his name.)

224.	Nunnery.	
225.	Union-hall.	
226.	Nunish.	Pertaining to, or like a nun.
227.	Non-aqua.	Having nothing at all to do with water.
228.	Nineveh.	
229.	Ninepin.	One of nine upright pieces of wood to be knocked down in the game of ninepins.
230.	Names.	
231.	Nomad.	
232.	Nominee.	A person nominated for a position or office.
233.	No Ma'am.	
234.	Enamour.	To bring to life, to animate with love.
235.	Animal.	
236.	No mash.	(Imagine a saucepan which has just been emptied of mashed potatoes.)
237.	Unmake	
238.	Nymph.	A beautiful, mythological maiden, always young.
239.	Numb.	
240.	Nurse.	
241.	Narrate.	
242.	No run.	
243.	Norm.	A standard; a set pattern to be maintained.
244.	Narrower.	
245.	Nearly.	
246.	Nourish.	
247.	New York.	

248. Nerve.

249. Nearby.

250. Nails.

251. Nailed.

252. Nylon.

253. New Loam.   Freshly-turned rich and fertile soil.

254. Kneeler.

255. Nail-hole.

256. Knowledge.

257. Nailing.

258. Nullify.   To cancel, to neutralize, to quash.

259. Unlab.   To dismantle a scientific laboratory.

260. Niches.   Vertical recesses in a wall to contain
a statue.

261. Unshod.

262. Nation.

263. Unjam.

264. Injure.

265. Unshell.   To extract a living organism from its
shell.

266. Nosh shop.   (Imagine the school tuck-shop or
something similar.)

267. No Joke.   A 'joke' that falls flat.

268. Unshaved.

269. Unship.   (Imagine a great crowd of people being
ordered off a ship.)

270. Necks.

271. Naked.

272. Noggin.   A small mug and/or its contents.

273.	Income.	
274.	Anchor.	
275.	Nickel.	A grey metal related to cobalt; an American coin worth about 2½ n.p.
276.	No Cash.	(Imagine someone fumbling in his pockets in order to pay a restaurant bill.)
277.	Knocking.	
278.	Encave.	To confine to a dark place; to keep in a cave.
279.	Uncap.	(Imagine schoolboys stealing each others caps.)
280.	Nephews.	
281.	Nevada.	
282.	Uneven.	
283.	Unfirm.	
284.	Never.	
285.	Navel.	
286.	Knavish.	Having the characteristics of a roguish trickster; a deceitful and dishonest man.
287.	Invoke.	To address in prayer; to implore assistance or protection.
288.	Unfavourable.	
289.	Enfeeble.	To make extremely weak and unable to function.
290.	Nibs.	
291.	Unpod.	To take from the pod, as peas.
292.	New Pan.	(Imagine a brilliantly shiny frying pan.)
293.	New Beam.	(Imagine the first beam ever from the sun.)
294.	Neighbour.	

295. Nibble.

296. Nippish.

297. Unpack.

298. Unpaved.

299. Nabob.   A wealthy, luxurious person, especially
                one returned from India with a fortune.

300. Moses.

301. Mast.

302. Mason.   One who cuts, builds, and prepares
                with stone.

303. Museum.

304. Miser.

305. Missile.

306. Massage.

307. Mask.

308. Massive.

309. Mishap.

310. Midas.   The king who craved for gold.

311. Mid-day.

312. Maiden.

313. Madam.

314. Motor.

315. Medal.

316. Modish.   In the style of the current fashion.

317. Medic.

318. Midwife.

319. Mudpie.

320. Manse.   The home of a Presbyterian minister.

321. Mend.

322. Minion.   Favourite child, servant or animal; slave.

323. Minim.   A creature of the smallest size or importance; a musical note.

324. Manner.

325. Manila.

326. Manage.

327. Maniac.

328. Manful.   Brave, resolute, bold; with man's best qualities.

329. Monopoly.   The sole power of trading; exclusive possession; a popular board-game.

330. Maims.

331. Mammouth.

332. Mammon.   The Syrian God of riches; wordly wealth.

333. My Mum.

334. Memory.

335. Mammal.

336. My match.

337. Mimic.

338. Mummify.   To preserve the body by embalming.

339. Mump.

340. Mars.

341. Maraud.   To make a plunderous raid; to go about pilfering.

342. Marine.

343. Miriam.

344. Mirror.

345. Moral.

346. March.

347. Mark.

348. Morphia.   The narcotic principle of opium.

349. Marble.

350. Males.

351. Malt.

352. Melon.

353. Mile Man.

354. Miller.

355. Molehill.

356. Mulish.   (Imagine anything that is characteristic of a mule.)

357. Milk.

358. Mollify.   To soften, assuage, appease.

359. Mail-bag.

360. Matches.

361. Mashed.

362. Machine.

363. Mishmash.   A jumble; a hodge podge; a medley.

364. Major.

365. Mesh Lock.   (Imagine something like a gear cog meshing and locking, or a lock that operates by an intricate mesh.)

366. Magician.

367. Magic.

368. Much Force.

369. Much bent.

370. Mikes.

371. Mocked.

372. Mohican.

373. Make Muck.

374. Maker.

375. Meekly.

376. My cash.

377. Making.

378. Make Off.   To hurry away, as a thief from the scene.

379. Magpie.

380. Movies.

381. Mufti.   An expounder of Mohammedan law; civilian dress as opposed to uniform.

382. Muffin.

383. Movement.

384. Mayfair.

385. Muffle.

386. My Fish.

387. Maffick.   To celebrate uproariously.

388. Mauve Feet.

389. Movable.

390. Mopes.   Sulks; being dull or out of spirits.

391. Moped.   Having completed 390!

392. Embank.   To throw up a bank; protect by a bank.

393. Wampum.   Name for money-beads and shells used by North American Indians.

394. Empire.

395. Maple.

396. Ambush.

397.	Impact.	
398.	Impavid.	Fearless; bold; intrepid.
399.	Imbibe.	To drink in; absorb (often used of liquor).
400.	Recess.	
401.	Recite.	
402.	Raisin.	
403.	Resumé.	A summing up; a condensed statement; a summary.
404.	Racer.	
405.	Wrestle.	
406.	Rose-show.	
407.	Risk.	
408.	Receive.	
409.	Rasp.	To rub with a coarse file; to utter in a grating way.
410.	Raids.	
411.	Radiate.	
412.	Rattan.	Indian climbing palm with long, thin, many-jointed pliable stem.
413.	Redeem.	
414.	Radar.	(Imagine 'beaming in' on some object in the sky.)
415.	Rattle.	
416.	Radish.	
417.	Reading.	
418.	Ratify.	To settle, confirm, approve, establish.
419.	Rat Bait.	
420.	Reigns.	
421.	Rained.	

422.	Reunion.	
423.	Uranium.	A radio-active white metallic element.
424.	Runner.	
425.	Runnel.	A rivulet or gutter.
426.	Ranch.	
427.	Rank.	
428.	Run Off.	A deciding, final contest; a gutter or spillway.
429.	Rainbow.	
430.	Remus.	One of two brothers suckled by a wolf—one of the founders of Rome.
431.	Rammed.	
432.	Roman.	
433.	Remember.	
434.	Rammer.	An armoured point on the prow of a ship.
435.	Rommel.	Notorious German war leader.
436.	Rummage.	
437.	Remake.	
438.	Ramify.	To form branches or subdivisions or offshots.
439.	Ramp.	
440.	Roars.	
441.	Reared.	
442.	Rareness.	
443.	Rearman.	The last man in a column or file.
444.	Rarer.	
445.	Rarely.	
446.	Rare Show.	

447.	Rearing.	
448.	Rarefy.	To lessen the density or solidity of, especially air.
449.	Rarebit.	A dainty morsel; often applied to Welsh Rarebit—grilled cheese on toast.
450.	Release.	
451.	Railed.	
452.	Re-loan.	
453.	Realm.	
454.	Roller.	
455.	Reel Line.	(Imagine a fishing line tangled on its reel.)
456,	Relish.	
457.	Relic.	
458.	Relief.	
459.	Relapse.	
460.	Riches.	
461.	Reached.	
462.	Region.	
463.	Regime.	Mode, style, diet; form of government.
464.	Rasher.	
465.	Rachel.	
466.	Rejudge.	
467.	Raging.	
468.	Arch Foe.	(Imagine yourself as a knight with one giant foe among a number of others.)
469.	Reach up.	
470.	Racks.	
471.	Racket.	

472. Reckon.	
473. Requiem.	A service spoken or sung for the peace of the soul of a dead person.
474. Raker.	(Imagine a man who does nothing but rake gardens.)
475. Recall.	
476. Roguish.	
477. Rococo.	A highly ornamented and florid style in design.
478. Recover.	
479. Raek up.	Colloquialism meaning to injure seriously in sport.
480. Refuse.	Rubbish; garbage.
481. Raft.	
482. Raven.	
483. Reform.	
484. Reefer.	A short jacket worn by sailors; a marijuana cigarette.
485. Raffle.	
486. Ravage.	
487. Revoke.	A card player's failure to follow suit though he could.
488. Revive.	
489. Roofable.	
490. Rabies.	
491. Rabid.	Furious, violent, unreasoning, mad.
492. Ribbon.	
493. Ripe Melon.	
494. Raper.	
495. Rabble.	

496. Rubbish.

497. Rebuke.

498. Rebuff.

499. Republic.   A society of persons or animals with equality between members.

500. Lasses.

501. Last.

502. Lesson.

503. Lyceum.   A place for instruction and lectures; A place in Athens where Aristotle taught.

504. Laser.   A super-concentrated beam of light coming from a substance which is vibrated.

505. Lazily.

506. Alsatian.

507. Lacing.

508. Lucifer.

509. Lisp.

510. Ladies.

511. Lighted.

512. Latin.

513. Late Meal.

514. Ladder.

515. Ladle.

516. Old-Age.

517. Leading.

518. Old Foe.

519. Lead Pipe.

520. Lance.

521. Land.

522. Linen.

523. Liniment.

524. Linear.

525. Lineal.   Relating to a line or lines; in direct line.

526. Launch.

527. Lank.

528. Luna Flight.

529. Line-up.

530. Looms.

531. Limit.

532. Layman.

533. Lame Mare.

534. Lamarck.   Famous French Zoologist and botanist.

535. Lamella.   A thin plate, especially of tissue or bone.

536. Lime Juice.

537. Looming.

538. Lymph.   Virus-laden matter obtained from a
                      diseased body.

539. Lamp.

540. Layers.

541. Lard.

542. Learn.

543. Alarm.

544. Leerer.

545. Laurel.

546. Large.

547. Lark.

548. Larva.

549. Larrup.   Colloquial for 'to thrash'.

550. Lilies.

551. Lilt.

552. Lowland.

553. Lielow Mattress.   A camping mattress which serves as a bed.

554. Lowlier.

555. Lily-livered.

556. Liliaceous.   Relating to the lily family; like a lily.

557. Lilac.

558. Low life.

559. Lullaby.

560. Lashes.

561. Legit.   Colloquial for that which is honest or 'above board'.

562. Legion.

563. Lush Meadow.

564. Lecher.

565. Lushly.

566. All-Jewish.

567. Logic.

568. Low shot.

569. Lush Pea.

570. Lakes.

571. Licked.

572. Lagoon.

573. Locum.   Colloquial for a deputy in any office, especially a doctor.

574. Lacquer.

575. Local.

576. Luggage.

577. Licking.

578. Liquefy. To bring a solid or a gas into a liquid condition.

579. Lock-up.

580. Leaves.

581. Livid.

582. Elfin. Like, or relating to, a fairy or an elf.

583. Alluvium. Soil deposited or washed down by the action of water

584. Lever.

585. Level.

586. Lavish.

587. Leaving.

588. Leave Off!

589. Life-boat.

590. Lips.

591. Leaped.

592. Lib Now! (Imagine this phrase as a Woman's Liberation placard.)

593. Labium. The floor of the mouth of insects and crustaceans etc.

594. Labour.

595. Label.

596. Lipchap. A cold sore on the lip.

597. Law-book.

598. Leap-frog.

599. Lap-up.

600. Chases.

601. Chaste.

602. Jason.   And the Golden Fleece!

603. Chessman.

604. Chaser.

605. Chisel.

606. Cheese-Show.

607. Chasing.

608. Joseph.

609. Jasper.   An opaque variety of quartz, usually red, yellow or brown.

610. Shades.

611. Shaded.

612. Jetton.   An engraved disc or counter.

613. Chatham.   Naval town in Kent.

614. Chatter.

615. Chattel.   A movable possession; property which is not freehold.

616. Chit-chat.

617. Cheating.

618. Shadoof.   A water raiser consisting of a long pole hung from a post, and a bucket or bottle.

619. Chat-up.   To talk to a person of the opposite sex with further contact in mind.

620. Chains.

621. Chant.

622. Genuine.

623. Chinaman.

624. Joiner.

625. Channel.

626. Change.

627. Chink.

628. Geneva. Headquarters for certain United Nations organisations; Major city of Switzerland.

629. Shin-bone.

630. Chums.

631. Ashamed.

632. Showman.

633. Jemima. Boot with elastic sides, having no laces or clasps to fasten.

634. Chimera. A fire-breathing monster with a lion's head, a goat's body, and a dragon's tail.

635. Shameless.

636. Jimjams. Nervous fears; delirium tremens.

637. Jamaica.

638. Shameful.

639. Champ.

640. Cheers.

641. Chart.

642. Shrine.

643. Chairman.

644. Juror.

645. Churl. A surly, ill-bred man.

646. Charge.

647. Cherokee.　　North American Indian.

648. Giraffe.

649. Chirp.

650. Jealous.

651. Child.

652. Chilean.

653. Show-loom.　　(Imagine an exquisite antique weaving machine put on special display.)

654. Jailer.

655. Shallowly.　　In a manner not intellectual, or lacking in depth.

656. Geology.

657. Challenge.

658. Shelf.

659. Julep.　　A sweet preparation serving as a vehicle for nauseous medicines.

660. Judges.

661. Judged.

662. Jejune.　　Bare, meagre, empty, attenuated; void of interest.

663. Judgement.

664. Judger.

665. Jewishly.

666. Choo-choo-choo.　　An especially puffy steam engine!

667. Joshing.　　Good-natured leg-pulling or joking.

668. Jehoshaphat.　　A king of Israel.

669. Shoe Shop.

670. Checks.

671. Checked.

672. Chicken.

673. Checkmate.   A position in the game chess in which opponent's king is trapped. The end of the game.

674. Checker.

675. Chuckle.

676. Jokish.

677. Checking.

678. Chekhov.   Famous Russian Author of short stories and plays.

679. Jacob.

680. Chafes.   Excites or heats by friction; wears by rubbing.

681. Shaft.

682. Shaven.

683. Chief Mao.

684. Shaver.

685. Joyful.

686. Chiff Chaff.   One of the British warbling birds.

687. Chafing.

688. Shove Off!

689. Shaveable.

690. Chaps.

691. Chapter.

692. Japan.

693. Chapman.

694. Chopper.

695. Chapel.

696. Sheepish.

697. Chipping.

698. Sheepfold.

699. Shopboy.

700. Kisses.

701. Cast.

702. Casino.

703. Chasm.

704. Kisser.

705. Gazelle.

706. Kiss Owch!

707. Cash.

708. Cohesive.   With the quality of sticking together, said especially of 'sticky tape' and molecules.

709. Cusp.   The point at which two branches of a curve meet and stop; the pointed end, especially of a leaf.

710. Cats.

711. Cadet.

712. Cotton.

713. Gotham.   A typical foolish town; New York City.

714. Catarrh.   A discharge from the mucous membrane caused by a cold in the head; the condition resulting from this.

715. Cattle.

716. Cottage.

717. Coating.

718. Cadaver.   A corpse.

719. Cut-up.   Colloquial for 'knife fight' in which one or both antagonists are injured.

720. Cans.

721. Cant.   Affected, insincere speech; the fashion of speech of a sect; to speak with whining insincerity.

722. Cannon.

723. Economy.

724. Coiner.

725. Kennel.

726. Conjure.

727. Conk.   Colloquial for 'to bang on the head'.

728. Convey.

729. Canopy.   A covering over a bed or a throne.

730. Cameos.   Pieces of relief carving in stone and agate, etc. with colour-layers utilized to give background.

731. Comet.

732. Common.

733. Commemorate.

734. Camera.

735. Camel.

736. Gamish.   In a plucky or rumbustious mood; of the quality of birds of game.

737. Comic.

738. Comfy.

739. Camp.

740. Caress.

741. Card.

742. Corn.

743. Cram.

744. Career.

745. Carol. _____

746. Crash. _____

747. Crack. _____

748. Carafe.   A glass water or wine bottle for the eating table.

749. Carp.   To catch at small faults; a freshwater fish usually bred in ponds.

750. Class. _____

751. Clod. _____

752. Clan. _____

753. Clam. _____

754. Clear. _____

755. Galilee.   The porch or chapel at the entrance of a church.

756. Clash. _____

757. Clack. _____

758. Cliff. _____

759. Clip. _____

760. Cages. _____

761. Caged. _____

762. Cushion. _____

763. Cashmere.   A rich shawl, originally made at Cashmere in India.

764. Cashier. _____

765. Cajole.   To persuade or soothe by flattery, deceit, etc.

766. Co-Judge. _____

767. Catching. _____

768. Cageful. _____

769. Ketchup.   Tomato sauce.

770.	Cakes.	
771.	Cooked.	
772.	Cocoon.	
773.	Cucumber.	
774.	Cooker.	
775.	Cackle.	
776.	Quackish.	Like the call of the duck; characteristic of a charlatan, imposter or pretender.
777.	Cooking.	
778.	Quickfire.	
779.	Cockup.	Colloquial for that which has been made a mess of; improperly arranged.
780.	Cafes.	
781.	Craved.	
782.	Coffin.	
783.	Caveman.	
784.	Caviar.	A food delicacy; the prepared roe of the sturgeon.
785.	Cavil.	To find objection or needless fault with.
786.	Gaffish.	Similar to a barbed fishing spear.
787.	Caving.	
788.	Cavafy.	The 'old poet' of Alexandria.
789.	Coffee Bar.	
790.	Cabs.	
791.	Cupid.	
792.	Cabin.	
793.	Cabman.	
794.	Caper.	To frolic, skip or leap lightly, as a lamb; a small berry used for making pickles and condiments.

795. Cable.

796. Cabbage.

797. Coping.

798. Keep Off.

799. Cobweb.

800. Faces.

801. Fast.

802. Pheasant.

803. Face Mole.

804. Visor.

805. Facile.

806. Visage.

807. Facing.

808. Phosphor.   Related to that which glows or phosphoresces.

809. Face Up.   Colloquial for 'meet the brunt'; accept the challenge or consequences.

810. Fates.   The three Greek godesses of Destiny.

811. Faded.

812. Fatten.

813. Fathom.

814. Fetter.

815. Fatal.

816. Fattish.

817. Fading.

818. Fateful.

819. Football.

820. Fans.

821. Faint.

822.	Finance.	
823.	Venom.	
824.	Fawner.	An obsequious or sycophantic person; one who insincerely praises for reward.
825.	Final.	
826.	Finish.	
827.	Fawning.	A deer giving birth.
828.	Fanfare.	
829.	Vain Boy.	
830.	Famous.	
831.	Vomit.	
832.	Famine.	
833.	Fame-Mad.	
834.	Femur.	The thigh bone.
835.	Female.	
836.	Famish.	
837.	Foaming.	
838.	Fumeful.	
839.	Vamp.	Adventuress; woman who exploits men; unscrupulous flirt.
840.	Farce.	
841.	Fort.	
842.	Fern.	
843.	Farm.	
844.	Farrier.	A man who shoes horses or treats them for disease.
845.	Frail.	
846.	Fresh.	

847. Frock.

848. Verify.   Establish the truth of, bear out, make good.

849. Verb.   (Imagine a word in action itself!)

850. False.

851. Fault.

852. Flan.   Pastry spread with jam or conserves.

853. Flame.

854. Flare.

855. Flail.   Wooden staff at the end of which a short heavy stick hangs swinging—for threshing.

856. Flash.

857. Flake.

858. Fluff.

859. Flab.

860. Fishes.

861. Fished.

862. Fashion.

863. Fishman.

864. Fisher.

865. Facial.

866. Fish-shop.

867. Fishing.

868. Fishfood.

869. Fishbait.

870. Focus.

871. Faked.

872. Fecund.   Prolific; fertile.

873. Vacuum.

874. Fakir.   A Mohammedan or Hindu religious devotee.

875. Fickle.

876. Fake China.

877. Faking.

878. Havocful.   'Filled' with devastation and destruction.

879. Vagabond.

880. Fifes.

881. Vivid.

882. Vivien.

883. Fife-man.

884. Fever.

885. Favillous.   Consisting of, or pertaining to, ashes.

886. Fifish.   Resembling, or having the characteristics of a fife.

887. Fifing.

888. Vivify.   Give life to; enliven; animate.

889. Viviparous.   Bringing forth young alive rather than as eggs.

890. Fibs.

891. Fibbed.

892. Fabian.   Employing cautious strategy to wear out an enemy.

893. Fob-maker.

894. Fibre

895. Fable.

896. Foppish.

897. Fee back.   (Imagine yourself receiving money you had paid for a product that was unsatisfactory.)

898.	Fob File.	
899.	Fab Boy.	Colloquialism for a young boy considered very attractive by girls.
900.	Basis.	
901.	Bast.	The inner bark of lime; other flexible fibrous barks.
902.	Basin.	
903.	Bosom.	
904.	Bazaar.	
905.	Puzzle.	
906.	Beseech.	To ask earnestly for; to entreat, supplicate or implore.
907.	Basic.	
908.	Passive.	
909.	Baseball.	
910.	Beads.	
911.	Bedded.	
912.	Button.	
913.	Bottom.	
914.	Batter.	
915.	Battle.	
916.	Badge.	
917.	Bedding.	
918.	Beatify.	To make happy or blessed; to declare that a person is blessed with eternal happiness.
919.	Bad Boy.	
920.	Bans.	Curses; interdicts; prohibitions; sentence of outlawry,
921.	Band.	

922.	Banana.	
923.	Benumb.	To make numb or torpid, insensible or powerless.
924.	Banner.	
925.	Banal.	Trivial, trite, stale, commonplace.
926.	Bannish.	
927.	Bank.	
928.	Banf.	A mountainous area in western Canada in the Rocky Mountains famous for its beauty and excellent skiing slopes.
929.	Pin up.	
930.	Beams.	
931.	Pomade.	A scented ointment, originating from apples, for the hair and skin of the head.
932.	Bemoan.	Weep or express sorrow for or over; to lament or bewail.
933.	Beam Maker.	
934.	Bemire.	To get stuck in wet mud.
935.	Pommel.	A rounded knob, especially at the end of a swordhilt; to beat with the fists.
936.	Bombshell.	
937.	Beaming.	
938.	Bumf.	Odds and ends; disorganised stuff; waste; rubbish.
939.	Bump.	
940.	Brass.	
941.	Bread.	
942.	Barn.	
943.	Brim.	

944. Barrier.

945. Barrel.

946. Barge.

947. Bark.

948. Brief.

949. Bribe.

950. Blaze.

951. Bald.

952. Balloon.

953. Blame.

954. Boiler.

955. Balliol.   One of the famous Colleges at Oxford.

956. Blush.

957. Black.

958. Bailiff.   A king's representative in a district; agent or lord of a manor; officer under a sheriff.

959. Bulb.

960. Beaches.

961. Budget.

962. Passion.

963. Pyjamas.

964. Poacher.   One who tresspasses to steal game or fish; a vessel for poaching eggs.

965. Bushel.   An 8-gallon measure for grain and fruit.

966. Push Chair.

967. Bushwack.   Dweller in the backwoods; guerrilla or bandit.

968. Bashful.

969.	Bishop.	
970.	Bacchus.	The Greek God of wine.
971.	Bucket.	
972.	Bacon.	
973.	Becalm.	To still; to make quiet; delay through lack of wind, as a yacht.
974.	Baker.	
975.	Buckle.	
976.	Baggage.	
977.	Backing.	Support, moral or physical; a web of strong material at the back of some woven fabric.
978.	Back Off.	
979.	Back Up.	
980.	Beehives.	
981.	Buffet.	
982.	Buffoon.	A wag, jester, mocker, a droll clown.
983.	Pavement.	
984.	Beaver.	
985.	Baffle.	
986.	Beefish.	
987.	Bivouac.	A temporary encampment without tents.
988.	Push Off.	
989.	Puff Up.	
990.	Babies.	
991.	Puppet.	
992.	Baboon.	
993.	Pipe Major.	

994. Paper.

995. Babble.

996. Baby Show.

997. Popgun.

998. Pipeful.

999. Pop Up.   An automatic toaster; a toy consisting
                of a lidded box with sprung puppet.

1000. Diseases.

This has been a giant chapter, but its importance is beyond question. The major system can be used, like the smaller systems, to remember short lists. Its advantage of course is that it is limitless.

It can therefore be used to store information. For example if you wish to remember a certain list of facts to which you would have to refer continually over a period of years you could memorise that list using the key words from, for example, 400 to 430. In this way you can build up a permanent library of important or interesting facts which you will never forget!

The major system is *not only* a peg system. It is also the basis for remembering numbers, dates and telephone numbers, etc., and to these we shall shortly turn.

CHAPTER ELEVEN

CARD MEMORY SYSTEM

Magicians and memory experts often amaze and amuse audiences with their ability to remember complete packs of cards in the order in which they were presented. They similarly astound their audiences by being able to rattle off, without any difficulty, the six or seven cards not mentioned when an incomplete 'pack' is randomly presented. Extraordinary as these feats may seem, they are not all that difficult and are usually quite straightforward—even though many people accuse the performer of having hidden assistants in the audience, marked cards, and a number of other tricks!

The system for remembering a complete pack of cards is similar in concept to the peg systems so far discussed. All that is necessary is to know the first letter of the word for the suit and the number of the card in that suit.

For example, all words for the club cards will begin with c, all words for the hearts with h, all words for the spades with s, and all the words for the diamonds with d. The second consonant for the card-word will be the consonant represented by the letter from the Major Memory System.

Taking as an example the 5 of spades we know that it must begin with 's' because it is a spade card, and that its last consonant must be 'l' because it is the 5, and 5 is represented by 'l'. Without much difficulty we arrive at the word 'sale' which represents the 5 of spades.

Taking another example, we wish to devise a word for the 3 of diamonds. The word must begin with 'd' because it is the diamond suit and its final consonant must be 'm' because 'm' is represented by the number 3 in the major system. Filling in with the first vowel we arrive at the word 'dam' which is our image word for the 3 of diamonds.

Following is a list of the cards (aces count as 'one') and their memory words. A few of the variations I will explain when you have had a chance to familiarise yourself with the list.

Clubs	Diamonds
CA—Cat	DA—Date
C2—Can	D2—Dane
C3—Cam	D3—Dam
C4—Car	D4—Deer
C5—Call	D5—Dale
C6—Cage	D6—Dash
C7—Cake	D7—Deck
C8—Cafe	D8—Dive
C9—Cab	D9—Dab
C10—Case	D10—Daze
CJ—Cadet	DJ—Dead wood
CQ—Cotton	DQ—Deaden
CK—Club	DK—Diamond

Hearts	Spades
HA—Hat	SA—Sot
H2—Hen	S2—Son
H3—Ham	S3—Sum
H4—Hair	S4—Sore
H5—Hail	S5—Sale
H6—Hash	S6—Sash
H7—Hag	S7—Sack
H8—Hoof	S8—Sage
H9—Hub	S9—Sap
H10—Haze	S10—Seas
HJ—Headed	SJ—Sated
HQ—Heathen	SQ—Satan
HK—Heart	SK—Spade

In this system the jacks and queens have been counted as the numbers 11 and 12, and 10 as 's', and the king simply as the name of the suit in which he resides. The memory words for the clubs are in many cases the same as those for the major system words for the 70's, but this need not concern you, as the two lists will never come into conflict.

How does the memory expert dazzle his audience? The answer is quite simple—whenever a card is called out he immediately associates that card with the appropriate number on his major system (*you* will of course be able to use *two* systems for this task, as the Skipnum system also contains enough pegs to hold a full pack of cards.).

If for example the first card called out was the 7 of diamonds you would associate the word 'deck' with the first word on your major system which is 'tea'. You might imagine the entire deck of a boat being covered in tea, or perhaps even the Boston Tea Party! If the next card called were the ace of hearts you would associate the word for this card—'hat'—with the second word on you memory system 'Noah' and would link these two. You could imagine Noah on the ark wearing an enormous rain-hat in order to keep off the flood! If the next card called were the queen of spades you would associate the word for that card —'satan'—with your third major system word 'Ma'. You could imagine your mother bashing satan over the head!

From these few examples I hope you can see how easy it can be to memorise an entire pack of cards in whatever order they happen to be presented to you. It is a most impressive feat to be able to perform in front of your friends.

Your facility in remembering cards can be taken a step further. It is possible to have someone randomly read you the names of all the cards in the deck, leaving out any six or seven he chooses. Without much hesitation you can tell him which cards these were!

There are two ways of doing this, the first being to use a technique similar to that explained in Chapter 8.

Whenever a card is called out you associate the image word for that card within a larger concept such as the block of ice previously mentioned. In different situations you can use a coal-cellar or a boat etc. as that in which you contain your card memory word. When all the cards have been presented you simply run down the list of card memory words noting those words which are *not* connected with the larger memory concept.

If the 4 of clubs had been called you might have pictured a car slithering across the huge cube of ice, or being trapped within it. You could hardly forget this image but if the card 4 of clubs had *not* been called you would immediately remember that you had *nothing* to remember.

The other system for this type of feat is to mutate or change in some way the card memory word if that card is called. For example if the king of clubs were called and your image for this was a cave-man like club you would imagine it being broken in half. Or if the card called were the 2 of hearts and your normal image for this was a simple farm hen you might imagine it with an extraordinarily large tail or with its head cut off!

The systems described in this chapter are basic to the remembering of cards, but it does not take much to see that in the actual playing of card games, a memory system such as this can be of enormous help. You have probably watched people repeating over and over to themselves the cards which they know have been put down or which are in other players' hands, and you have probably seen them sigh with exasperation at their inability to remember accurately!

With your new memory system such tasks will become only too simple.

CHAPTER TWELVE

LONG NUMBER MEMORY SYSTEM

Give a long number such as 95862190377 to someone to remember and he will try: to repeat it as you present it to him, eventually getting bogged down in his own repetition; to subdivide it into two-or-three number groups, eventually losing the order and content of these; to work out mathematical relations between the numbers as you present them, inevitably getting confused; or to 'picture' the number as it is presented, the photograph in his mind always becoming blurred!

If you think back to the initial test in which you were asked to perform a feat like this, you will probably recall your own approach.

Remembering long numbers is really quite simple if you apply the Major System. Instead of using this system as a word system to remember objects, it is possible to use the basic words of the system itself to recall the numbers from which they are made.

Let us take the number at the top of the page. It is composed of: 95—ball
86—fish
21—net
90—base
37—mac
7—key

In order to remember this almost impossible number all that we now have to do is to link the key words which relate to sub-sections of that number.

The image-chain here could be of a large *ball* bouncing off the head of a *fish* which has just broken out of a *net* and fallen to the *base* level of the pier where it struck a man wearing a *mac* who was bending over to pick up his *key*.

Recalling these words and transforming them to numbers we get:

b—9
l—5

f—8
sh—6
n—2
t—1
b—9
s—0
m—3
c—7
k—7
95862190377!

There is no need, of course, to remember these large numbers by taking groups of two. It is just as easy, and sometimes more easy, to consider groups of three. Let us try this with the number 851429730584. It is composed of:

851—fault
429—rainbow
730—cameos
584—lever

In order to remember this number, which is slightly longer than the previous number, it is once again a matter of linking our key words.

We could imagine a force which caused a break or *fault* in *rainbow* coloured *cameos* which are so heavy they needed a *lever* to move them.

Recalling these words and transforming them we get:

f—8
l—5
t—1
r—4
n—2
b—9
c—7
m—3
s—0
l—5
v—8
r—4
851429730584!

A further system for remembering numbers such as this, especially if you have not committed the major system entirely to memory, is to make up four-consonant words from the number you have to remember. Let us try this with a 16 digit number: 1582907191447620. From the digits we get 1582—*telephone*, 9071—*basket*, 9144—*botherer*, 7620—*cushions*. Our image chain can be of a *telephone* being thrown into a basket where an annoying person (a *botherer !*) has also been thrown with some *cushions*. Recalling the number should by now be a familiar process to you.

To check on the amazing difference this method of number memorisation makes, go back to the original test-chapter and see how easy those initial numbers were!

CHAPTER THIRTEEN

TELEPHONE NUMBER MEMORY SYSTEM

Most people 'just can't' remember telephone numbers. In order to overcome this disability they employ all kinds of elaborate systems, ranging from the person who keeps card files of the numbers he needs to remember and carries these around with him, to the one who jots down numbers on odd pieces of paper and is continually ringing the wrong person.

Remembering telephone numbers is not difficult at all as long as we remember the number-letter correspondence from the Major System. All that is necessary is to substitute a letter for the number we wish to remember. Having done this, we make up association words that link the number to the person.

Let us try this with the ten people from the initial test:

Your local butcher	329–8737
Your dentist	298–9107
Your bank manager	770–5323
Your doctor	321–3989
Your local grocer	455–8801
Your local chemist	833–9939
Your tennis partner	539–4112
Your plumber	211–8519
Your local pub	939–1427
Your garage	147–9340

The butcher's number—329–8737—starts with the numbers '329' which translate in letters to 'm', 'n' and 'b'. These letters can be remembered in a variety of ways, but the one which springs immediately to mind is: 'My Neighbourhood Butcher'. The remaining four numbers we have to deal with are '8737' which can be converted to 'v or f', 'k, c, g', 'm' and 'k, c, g'. Our task here is to make up either one word which contains these letters in order, two short words which also contain these letters in order, or four words, the initial letter of which represents the number we are trying to remember. In the case of the butcher the last of these choices is probably the best. We select v, g, m, and hard c to give us 'Very Good Meat Cuts'. We could of course, substitute 'Fairly' for 'Very' and 'Gory' for 'Good' etc.

As practice on these items is always important, take a quick look again at the people and their numbers, noting the letters. Briefly try to make up memory words or phrases for the ten telephone numbers, and when you have practiced them, consider the following suggestions for each one:

Your dentist—298-9107. The initial numbers translate to the letters 'NPF'. These letters could form the phrase 'Needles Produce Fear'. The remaining four letters we have to choose from are (9107) 'p, b', 't, d', 's, z, or soft c', and 'k, g, hard c'. One two-word combination that we might use for this is 'Bad Suck' because people with toothaches often tend to suck at the painful tooth. A four word suggestion of a more positive nature is 'Pain Does Certainly Go' (or 'Come' if you still feel none too kindly toward your dentist!)

Your bank manager—770-5323. The first three numbers translate to the letters 'hard c, g', and 's'. This can be conveniently converted to the three keywords 'Cash, Gold and Silver'. The remaining four numbers translate to the letters 'l', 'm', 'n', 'm', which can often be truthfully translated into 'Lent Me No Money!'

Your doctor—321-3989. The initial three numbers translate to the letters 'm', 'n', 'd', easily forming the phrase 'My Nice Doctor'. The following four numbers translate to 'm', 'p or b', 'f or v', and 'p or b'. An obvious linking phrase here being 'Makes Pain feel Better'.

Your local grocer—455-8801. The initial letters translate into 'f', 'l', 'l', fitting neatly into the phrase 'Fresh Leafy Lettuces'. The latter four numbers translate to the letters 'f, v', 'f, v,' 's, z, soft c', and 't, d, th'. An appropriate phrase from this selection could be 'Very Fine Celery And Tomatoes'. The initial word could be changed to 'Fairly' or 'Few' and the second to 'Foul'.

Your local chemist—833-9939. The initial numbers translate to the letters 'f', 'm', 'm'. These could be used to form the phrase 'For Medical Materials'. The remaining four numbers translate to 'p, b', 'p, b' 'm' and 'p, b'. A suggested four word phrase here is 'Potions, Poisons, Medicines and Pills'.

Your tennis partner—539–4112. The initial numbers translate to the letters 'l', 'm' and 'b'. An appropriate phrase might be 'Lobs Many Balls'. The remaining four numbers translate to the letters 'r', 't, d, th', 't, d, th', and 'n'. Our memory phrase here might be 'Rarely Touches The Net'.

Your plumber—211–8519. Here the initial three numbers translate to 'n', 'd', 'd'. This can be conveniently combined in the single keyword 'NeeDeD'. The remaining four numbers translate to the letters 'f, v', 'l', 't, d, th' and 'p, b'. Our memory phrase could either be 'Fixes Leaks, Drips and Plumbing' or 'Faulty Lines, Taps and Pipes'.

Your local pub—939–1427. The initial three numbers translate to the letters 'p', 'm', 'b'. Which can be used to form such three-letter phrases as 'Publicans Manage Beer'. The remaining four numbers translate to 't, d, th', 'r', 'n', and 'k, g hard c.' In this case there is no need to make up a phrase—we can contain it all in the one word 'Drunk'!

Your garage—147–9340. Again the first three numbers, which translate to the letters 't', 'r', 'k', can be combined in the single and appropriate keyword 'TRucK'. The remainder of the number translates to 'p, b', 'm', 'r' and 's, z, soft c'. This can be put into the phrase 'Broken Motor Repair Service'.

The examples given above are of course very particular, and it will now be up to you to apply the system outlined to the telephone numbers which are important to *you* to remember.

In some cases the combination of numbers may present a greater than usual difficulty, and 'appropriate' phrases or words may be almost impossible to devise. In such cases the solutions are still fairly simple.

In the first case, you may make up inappropriate words out of the numbers you have to deal with, and then use the basic system, making absurd and exaggerated images which you link with the person whose telephone number you are trying to remember.

For example, if the telephone number of one of your friends whose hobby is cricket is 411–4276 you would take the Major System word for 41 which is 'rat', the Major word for 142 which is 'drain', and the Major word for 76 which is 'cage'. Your image for remembering this number would be of your friend swatting a *rat* instead of a cricket ball and of the rat flying through the air landing in a *drain*, the iron grill of which is similar to the bars of a *cage*!

133

The telephone number memory system is easy and enjoyable to practice, once you have mastered it. As with all other systems, it requires practice, so before you proceed to the next chapter you are advised to have committed to memory at least a few numbers which are important to you.

CHAPTER FOURTEEN

MEMORY SYSTEM FOR SCHEDULES AND APPOINTMENTS.

As with telephone numbers, many people find appointments and schedules hard to remember. They employ similar systems for coping with their problem, the most common, of course, being the diary. Unfortunately many people don't always keep their diaries with them!

In this chapter I introduce two systems, the first of which is for immediate daily use, the second for remembering schedules and appointments for an entire week.

The first involves your basic peg systems. Simply equate the number in your system with the hour of your appointment. Since there are 24 hours in a day, you can either join the shorter system together, with an appropriate total of 24, or use the first 24 peg words in one of the larger systems.

Let us assume you have the following appointments:

> 7—Early morning training
> 10—Dentist
> 1—Luncheon
> 6—Board meeting
> 10—Late film

We will assume that you are using the Skipnum system to remember these appointments. At the beginning of the day, which in this case will certainly be no earlier than 5.30 a.m., you run through the list and check for words with associations.

7 a.m., represented by the word *egg*, is the time for your Early Morning Group Athletic Practice. Imagine your whole team running on eggshells, or enjoying a breakfast of egg before or after.

At 10 a.m. (toast) you have an appointment with the dentist. Imagine all your teeth sinking into a piece of *toast* which causes pain.

Your next appointment, at 1 p.m. (13.00) is for lunch. The

key word is 'tea'. Imagine the rather depressing prospect of a lunch at which nothing but tea is served.

At 6 p.m. you have a Board Meeting. The Skipnum memory word for 18 (18.00 hours equals 6 p.m.) is 'tape'. The association here is not difficult—imagine the confidential matters of your Board Meeting being tape-recorded on an enormous machine.

Finally you have an appointment at 10 p.m. (2200 hours) to see a late film. The Skipnum key word is 'troop'. Imagine the audience of which you will be a part as a well organised military force!

The second system for remembering schedules and appointments may be used for an entire week. As with the memory system for dates, take Sunday as day 1 of the week and ascribe a number to each of the other days:

Sunday	— 1
Monday	— 2
Tuesday	— 3
Wednesday	— 4
Thursday	— 5
Friday	— 6
Saturday	— 7

Having given a number to the day, we treat the hours as they are treated in the small system discussed above, and as they appear in railway, shipping and airline schedules. The day is considered to have 24 hours, from 2400 (midnight) through 1 a.m. (0100), noon (1200), 1 p.m. (1300) and back to midnight (2400).

Thus for any hour and day of the week a two- or three-digit number is formed—day first, hour second. All that is necessary is to transfer the number into the word of the major system list. Having arrived at the word we link it with the appropriate appointment.

Supposing you had an appointment to see a car you wanted to buy at 9.00 a.m. on Tuesday. Tuesday is represented by the number 3 which in the major system translates to the letter 'm'. The hour, 9, translates to the letter 'b,p'. Referring to the basic list we see that the key word for Tuesday at 9.00 a.m. is 'map'. To remember this appointment you might imagine the car you are going to see either bursting through a giant map, wrapped in a giant map, or driving across a giant map.

As another example, suppose you have an appointment for a guitar lesson at 5.00 p.m. (hour number 17) on a Thursday (day number 5). The number we derive from Thursday at 5.00 p.m. is 517, the word for this being 'leading'. To remember this, imagine yourself leading an entire orchestra with your solo guitar!

You may think this system a bit cumbersome, because it requires a fairly thorough knowledge of the larger numbers in the Major System, but this can be overcome by 'rotating' the hours of the day to suite those hours in which you have most appointments. If, for example, your day does not usually start until 10.00 a.m., then 10.00 a.m. can be considered to be number 1 in your appointment memory system. In this manner the most important and often-used hours in your day will nearly always be represented by only 2-digit numbers, i.e. the numbers from 10 to 100 in the Major System.

CHAPTER FIFTEEN

MEMORY SYSTEM FOR DATES IN OUR CENTURY

When you have finished this chapter you will be able to give the correct day of the week for any date between the years 1900 to the present!

Two systems may be used, the first of which is faster and simpler and applies to only one given year while the second spans many years and is a little harder. These systems owe much to Harry Lorayne, a well-known North American memory expert.

Using the first of these systems, let us assume that we wish to know the day for any given date in the year 1971. In order to accomplish what may sound like a rather considerable feat, all that is necessary is to remember (or jot down) the following number:

377426415375

'Rubbish!' you might say, but when this system is explained you will see that it is in fact very clear and easy to operate. The individual digits of the 12-digit number represent the first Sunday for each month of the year 1971. The first Sunday in April, for example falls on the 4th day of the month, the first Sunday in December falls on the 5th day of the month, and so on.

Once you have remembered this number, and I recommend that you remember it in the way that was explained in the Long Number memory system chapter, you will rapidly be able to calculate the day of the week for any date in the year.

It is best to explain this concept with examples, so let us assume that your birthday fell on April 28th, and that you wished to know what day the date represented. Taking the 4th digit from your memory number you would realise that the first Sunday fell on the 4th. By the process of adding sevens to this initial Sunday date you rapidly calculate that the second Sunday of the month fell on the 11th ($4 + 7 = 11$); the third

Sunday of the month fell on the 18th (11 + 7 = 18) and that the last Sunday of the month fell on the 25th. Knowing this you recite the remaining dates and the days of the week until you arrive at the date in question: April 26th = Monday; April 27th = Tuesday; April 28th = Wednesday. In other words your birthday falls on a Wednesday in the year 1971!

Suppose you wish to know the final day of the year. The process is similar. Knowing that the 1st Sunday of the last month falls on the 5th day you add the three sevens representing the following Sundays to arrive at Sunday 26th. Reciting the next few dates and days we get: 27th Monday; 28th Tuesday; 29th Wednesday; 30th Thursday; 31st (the last day of the year.) a Friday.

As you can see this system can be applied to any year for which you may especially need to know days for dates. All you have to do is to make up a memory number for the first Sunday, or for that matter the first Monday, Tuesday, etc. of each month of the year, add sevens where appropriate to bring you near to the day in question, and recite to that day.

An interesting and quick way to make use of the memory number of one year with relation to surrounding years is to realise that with each year the first date for the days at the beginning of the month goes down one, with the exception of leap years when the extra day produces a jump of two for the following year. In the years 1969, 1970, 1971 for instance the first Sunday for January in each of those years fell respectively on the 5th, 4th, and 3rd days of the month.

The second of the two systems to be introduced in this chapter is for calculating the day for any date from 1900 to the present. It is necessary in this system to ascribe to each month a number which will always remain the same. The numbers for the months are as follows:

January	—	1
February	—	4
March	—	4
April	—	0
May	—	2
June	—	5
July	—	0
August	—	3
September	—	6

October	—	1
November	—	4
December	—	6

Some people suggest that these be remembered using associations such as January is the first month, the fourth letter in February is r which represents 4, and so on but I think that it is better to use the number:

144025036146

making the words *drawer*, *snail*, *smash* and *tired*. These can then be linked by imagining a drawer on which a snail with a very hard shell is eventually smashed after an effort which made you tired. In this way the key numbers for the months can be remembered.

In addition to the key numbers for the months the years themselves have key numbers and I have listed them from 1900 to 1984, after which date, according to George Orwell, memory will be 'taken care of!'.

0	1	2	3	4	5	6
1900	1901	1902	1903	1909	1904	1905
1906	1907	1913	1908	1915	1910	1911
1917	1912	1919	1914	1920	1921	1916
1923	1918	1924	1925	1926	1927	1922
1928	1929	1930	1931	1937	1932	1933
1934	1935	1941	1936	1943	1938	1939
1945	1940	1947	1942	1948	1949	1944
1951	1946	1952	1953	1954	1955	1950
1956	1957	1958	1959	1965	1960	1961
1962	1963	1969	1964	1971	1966	1967
1973	1968	1975	1970	1982	1977	1972
1979	1974	1980	1976		1983	1978
1984			1981			

How does this system work? Well, for once the answer is that it is not completely easy although with a little practice it can become almost second nature. The method is as follows, given the month, numerical date, and the year, you add the number represented by the month key to the number of the date, and add this total to the key number representing the year in question. From the total you subtract all the sevens, and the remaining number represents the day in the week, taking Sunday as day 1.

In order to check this system, we will take a couple of examples, one from a recent year, and one which if you have bought this book before the end of 1972, will be a day in the future.

The day we will try to hunt down is the 19th March, 1969. Our key number for March is 4 which we must then add to the date in question which is 19, $19 + 4 = 23$. To this total we must add the key number for the year 1969. Referring to the list we find that this is 2. Adding 2 to our previous total we arrive at $23 + 2 = 25$. Subtracting all the sevens from this $(3 \times 7 = 21)$ we arrive at $25 - 21 = 4$. The day in question is consequently the 4th day of the week which is a Wednesday!

The date in the future we shall be concerned with is August 23rd 1972. Our key number for August is 3 which we add to 23 giving 26. The key number for the year 1972 is 6 which added to 26 gives us a total of 32. Subtracting all the sevens $(4 \times 7 = 28)$ from 32 we arrive at 4. The 4th day of the week is a Wednesday which is the day for August 23rd, 1972!

The only exception to this rule occurs in leap years, and then only in the months of January and February. Your calculations will be identical but for these two months only the day of the week will be one day earlier than the day you calculate.

As with other systems the best way to gain confidence with those discussed in this chapter is to practise them. I suggest that you start with the easier of the two first, become skilled in it, and then graduate to the more advanced. Both of these systems are excellent for entertaining your friends and social acquaintances.

CHAPTER SIXTEEN

MEMORY SYSTEM FOR IMPORTANT HISTORICAL DATES

The two systems you have just learnt enable you to remember the day for any date in this century. The next system will assist you in the memorisation of significant dates in history.

In Chapter 1 the memory test included a list of 10 such dates. They were:

1. 1666 — Fire of London.
2. 1770 — Beethoven's birthday.
3. 1215 — Signing of Magna Carta.
4. 1917 — Russian Revolution.
5. c.1454 — First Printing Press.
6. 1815 — Battle of Waterloo.
7. 1608 — Invention of the telescope.
8. 1905 — Einstein's theory of Relativity.
9. 1789 — French Revolution.
10. 1776 — Declaration of American Independence.

The method for remembering these or any other such dates is simple, and is similar to the method for remembering telephone numbers.

All you have to do is to make a word or string of words from the letters which represent the numbers of the date. In most cases there is no point in including the one representing the thousand, as you know the approximate date in any case. Let us try this system on the dates above.

1. The Fire of London in 1666 virtually destroyed the city leaving it a heap of ashes. Our memory phrase for the date 1666 would thus be 'ashes, ashes, ashes!', or 'charred ashes generally'.

2. Beethoven is famous for many musical accomplishments, but among his greatest and perhaps most controversial was the 9th Symphony in which he included a choir. His style of music made full use of the percussion instruments. Knowing this,

remembering his birthday in 1770 becomes easy: 'Crashing Choral Symphony'.

3. The signing of the Magna Carta in 1215 marked a new age of sense and reason. To remember this date we can use the phrase 'New Document—Liberalisation'.

4. The Russian Revolution of 1917 was an uprising of the people against what they considered abnormal oppression. They demanded greater equality in the form of Communism. Our memory phrase: 'People Demand Communism'.

5. Printing presses are often great rotating machines that churn out thousands of pages a minute. We can imagine a small version of this as the first printing press, in approximately 1454, which can be remembered by the word 'RoLleR'.

6. The Battle of Waterloo in 1815 was triumphant for Wellington but can be considered fatal for Napoleon. Once again we use a memory word rather than a memory phrase to remember the date: 'FaTaL'.

7. The invention of the telescope by Galileo in 1608 changed the way in which man's eyes saw the sky. Our memory phrase: 'Changed Sky Focus'.

8. In 1905 Einstein's theory of relativity shed new light on the way in which matter and energy exist. His theory solved a number of puzzles that had occupied man, but also gave rise to many more. Our key word 'PuZZLe'.

9. In the French Revolution in 1789 the king was ranged against the people. Hence we remember the date by 'King Fights People'.

10. The declaration of American Indepencence in 1776 marked a new feeling of optimism and confidence in the American way of life. This can be encapsulated in the one word: 'CoCKSure'.

As you can see, the system for remembering important dates in history is a simple one and should make a task which most people find hard an enjoyable exercise in creative remembering.

CHAPTER SEVENTEEN

REMEMBERING BIRTHDAYS, ANNIVERSARIES AND DAYS AND MONTHS OF HISTORICAL DATES

This next system will be easy for you because it makes use of systems you have already learned. It is also easier than most other systems suggested for remembering such items, because the two large memory systems you have learned—Skipnum and the Major System—may be used together as 'keys' for the months and days (other systems usually require code names that have to be especially devised for the months).

The system works as follows: months are assigned the appropriate key word from the Major System.

January	—	Tea
February	—	Noah
March	—	Ma
April	—	Ray
May	—	Law
June	—	Jaw
July	—	Key
August	—	Poe
September	—	Pa
October	—	Toes
November	—	Tate
December	—	Tan

The days from 1 to 31 are assigned the appropriate word from the Skipnum system.

To remember a birthday, anniversary or historical date, all that is necessary is to form a linked image between the month- and day-words and the date you wish to remember.

For example, your girl-friend's birthday falls on November 1st. The key word from the Major System for November is 'tate'; and the key word from Skipnum for 'one' is 'up'. You imagine that your girl-friend is framed or hung *up* in the *Tate* Gallery.

The anniversary you wish to remember is your parent's Wedding Anniversary which falls on February 25th. The Major System key word for February is 'Noah'; the Skipnum key word for 25 is 'try'. Imagine Noah, who 'married' the pairs of animals, *try*ing to marry your parents at the same time.

Historical dates are just as easy to remember. For example the date when the United Nations came into formal existence was October 24th. The Major System key word for October is 'toes', and the Skipnum key word for 24 is 'trot'. We imagine the different shaped and coloured toes of representatives of the world's nations hurrying (trotting) to meet because of the urgency created by the end of the Second World War.

There is one small danger in this system, and this is epitomised by those people who don't forget the date—they forget to remember it! This can be overcome by making a habit of checking through, on a regular basis, your memory links for the coming one or two weeks.

The memory system outlined in this chapter can be effectively linked with the previous system for remembering historical dates by year. In this way you will have provided yourself with a *complete* date-remembering system.

CHAPTER EIGHTEEN

MEMORY SYSTEM FOR SPEECHES, JOKES, NARRATIVES, DRAMATIC PARTS AND POEMS, ARTICLES

The problems and embarrassments with the items listed in the title of this chapter are almost endless!

The speech maker, terrified that he will make a blunder in front of his audience, usually reverts to reading word-for-word from a prepared text, the result of which is inevitably a monotonous and de-personalised presentation. The slightly more courageous speech-maker will often commit his speech to memory, falling into the trap of scrambling through it as fast as possible in order to get to the end before he forgets something! In most cases *he does* forget something and the most awkward silences ensue as he gropes for the lost thread.

Similar, although not so important, situations arise in the telling of jokes. These are not so much embarrassing to the story teller as annoying to the person to whom the joke is being told. How familiar is the situation in which, after ages of build up, the story teller suddenly looks at you with a slack jaw and the exclamation 'Damn! I've forgotten the punch line, but anyway it was a *really* funny story'.

Dramatic parts present a different problem in that they are usually to be memorised by actors who have continual practise sessions with the same material. Their task is nevertheless still difficult, and each member of the group must make sure that his familiarity with the material is at least on a par with that of the other members. In more lengthy and difficult works, soliloquies and poems are among the items that have to be remembered, and the task becomes even more difficult.

Remembering articles is often necessary in an academic or business situation, embarrassment usually arising during exam time when the student 'knows that he knows' but just can't get the information off the tip of his tongue or his mind; and in the business situation where one is asked to discuss a report that everyone else has read, and either goes completely blank or cannot recall a major point.

These are the problems. How can they be solved? Unfortunately there is no *simple* system such as the Link and Peg systems discussed previously, but there are methods and techniques that make the remembering of this kind of material much easier. As the techniques vary slightly in different cases, I shall consider each individually.

Speeches

If you wish to make a good speech one of the cardinal rules is *never* to memorise it word for word. Another is *never* to read it.

1. Generally research the topic about which you are going to speak, making recordings of ideas, quotations and references which you think might prove relevant.

2. Having completed your basic research sit down and *plan out* the basic structure of your presentation. *Do not* start to write your speech before you have completed your basic design. I have known people who have written the 'same' speech seven times before arriving at their final draft. If they had organised themselves a little more adequately to begin with, *weeks* could have been saved.

3. With your basic structure in front of you fill in the details in note form so that you complete an outline which needs only grammatical and sentence structure changes to become a coherent presentation.

4. Practise making your speech from this completed outline. You will find that, having completed the research and having thought about the structure of the material, you will already have nearly memorised your speech. Initially, of course, there will be points at which you hesitate, but with a little practice you will find that not only do you know your speech, *you also know what you are talking about!*

This point is especially important, for it means that when you finally *do* speak to your audience you need have no fear of forgetting the word-order or what you are presenting. You simply say what you have to say, using the appropriate vocabulary and not a rigid succession of sentence structures. In other words, you become a *creative* rather than a static speaker. This is *Always* preferably.

5. As a precautionary step it is advisable to jot down on a

small card, or to remember on one of your smaller memory systems, the key words in the basic outline of your speech. This greatly reduces the possibility of forgetting.

The only problem you may consider still unsolved is that of not being able, immediately, to find the right word at the right time. Don't worry about this. When the audience senses that a speaker knows what he is talking about, an effective pause makes it obvious that he is creating on the platform. This *adds* rather than subtracts from the enjoyment of listening, for it makes the presentation less formal and more spontaneous.

Jokes and Narratives

Jokes and narratives are far easier to deal with than are speeches, because most of the creative work has already been done for you. The problem is nevertheless a two-fold one: first, you must remember the joke or narrative to begin with, and second, you must remember its details.

The first of these problems is easily solved by using a section of the major system as a permanent library for the stories you wish to file. I need go into this point no further, as it is simply a matter of selecting a key word and associating it with the key word of the System.

The second problem is slightly more difficult to overcome, and involves once again our use of the link system. Let us take, for example, the joke about the man who went to the pub and bought a pint of beer. Having bought this beer, he suddenly realised he had to make a telephone call, but knew that some of the 'characters' in the bar might well swipe his pint before he returned. In order to prevent this he wrote on his glass 'I am the World's Karate Champion.' and went to make his telephone call, securely thinking that his beer was safe.

When he returned he saw immediately that his glass was empty and noticed more scribbling underneath his own. It read 'I am the World's fastest runner—thanks!'

To remember this joke we *consciously* select key words from it, joining them into the basic narrative.

All we need from this full paragraph of narration are the words 'pint', 'phone', 'write', 'karate champion', and 'runner'. With these few words, which can be linked in whatever way we please, the whole sequence and essence of the joke will return immediately, and those horrible silences as one runs out of steam in the middle of a story need never recur!

Articles

Articles may need to be remembered on a very short-term basis or on a long-term basis, and the systems for remembering each are different.

If you have to attend a meeting or to make a brief resume of an article you have only recently read, you can remember it almost totally, and at the same time can astound your listeners by remembering the pages you are referring to. The method is simple: take one, two or three ideas from each page of the article and slot them on to one of your peg memory systems. If there is only one idea per page, you will know that when you are down to memory word 5 in your basic system, you are referring to the 5th page, whereas if there are two ideas per page and you are at memory word 5 you will know you are the top of page 3.

When an article has to be remembered over a longer period of time, we once again revert to the link system, taking key words from the article and linking them in such a way as to make them most memorable. This method of remembering will enable you not only to recall the sequence of the events and ideas but also to retain a more adequate general impression of what the article was about. The act of *consciously attempting to remember* is *itself* a part of learning.

Dramatic Parts and Poems

The last section of this chapter deals with those two items that have been in the past, and are still unfortunately today, the bane of the schoolchild.

The method usually employed (and recommended) is to read a line over and over again, 'get it'; read the next line, 'get it'; join the two together; 'get them'; read the next line and so on ad nausum until the first lines have been forgotten!

A system recommended and used successfully by well-known actors and actresses is almost the reverse. In this system the material to be remembered is read and re-read quickly but with understanding over a period of four days, approximately 5 times a day. In this manner the reader becomes far more familiar with the material than he realises and at the end of his 20th reading tries to recall, without looking at the text, the material to be remembered. Almost *without fail* the mind will have absorbed 90% or more totally, and remembering will have been a natural outgrowth of reading.

As I have said, this system has been found far more successful than the line-by-line repeating system, but even it can be improved considerably.

Once again the link system and key words come into play. If the material to be remembered is poetry, a few major key words will help the mind to 'fill in' the remaining words which will almost automatically fall into place between the key words.

If the material to be remembered is part of a script, once again key words and linking images can prove essential. The basic content of a long speech can be strung together with ease, and the cues from speaker to speaker can also be handled far more effectively. It is these cues that often cause chaos on the stage because of the silences and breaks in continuity that may occur when one performer forgets his last word or another forgets his first. If these last words (or even actions) are linked in the way that we link objects in our memory system, breaks and confusion can be completely avoided.

In summary, the remembering of speeches, narratives, jokes, articles, dramatic parts and poems involves a number of slightly differing techniques. In all cases, however, the use of some form of link, key words, and repetition is necessary.

CHAPTER NINETEEN

MEMORY SYSTEMS FOR LANGUAGES

When hearing the word 'language', some tend to think only of *foreign* languages. Seldom do they stop to think that the term includes their own tongue. The title of this chapter consequently refers to English as well as to other languages.

As I mentioned in my book *Speed Reading* vocabulary is considered to be the most important single factor not only in the development of efficient reading but also in academic and business success. This is not surprising when one realises that the size of one's vocabulary is usually an indication of the depth of one's knowledge.

Since vocabulary is the basic building block of language, it it desirable and necessary to develop methods of learning and remembering words more easily. One of the better ways of accomplishing this aim is to learn the prefixes (letters, syllables or words recurring before root words) the suffixes (letters, syllables or words recurring at the end of root words) and the roots (words from which others are derived) that occur most frequently in the language you are attempting to learn. A comprehensive list of these appears in the vocabulary chapters of my book *Speed Reading*.

Here are some more tips on how to improve your word memory:

1. Browse through a good dictionary, studying the ways in which the prefixes, suffixes and roots of the language are used. Whenever possible, use association to strengthen your recall.

2. Introduce a fixed number of new words into your vocabulary everyday. New words are retained only if the principle of *repetition*, as explained earlier, is practised. Use your new words in context and as many times as possible after you have initially learned them.

3. Consciously *look* for new words in the language. This directing of your attention, known as 'mental set', leaves the 'hooks' of your memory more open to catch new linguistic fish!

These are general learning aids to assist your memory in acquiring knowledge of a language. They may be applied to English, as a means for improving your present vocabulary, or to any foreign languages you are beginning to learn.

Having established a *general* foundation for learning words, let us be more specific in the remembering of *particular* words. As with other memory systems the key word is *association*. In the context of language-learning it is well to associate sounds, images and similarities, using the fact that certain languages are grouped in 'families' and have words that are related.

To give you an idea of this linking method, I shall consider a few words from English, French, Latin and German.

In English we want to remember the word 'vertigo' which means dizziness or giddiness, and in which a person feels as if he or surrounding objects are turning around. To imprint this word on the memory we associate the sound of it with the phrase 'where to go?' which is the kind of question you would ask if you felt that all surrounding objects were rotating about you! Two words which many people confuse in the English language are: 'acrophobia', which is a morbid fear of heights, and 'agoraphobia' which is a morbid fear of open spaces. The distinction can be firmly established if you associate the 'acro' in acrophobia with acrobat (a person who performs at great height!) and the 'agora' from agoraphobia with agriculture, bringing to mind images of large flat fields (though the Greek word actually means marketplace!).

Foreign languages are more 'approachable' when one realises that they form groups. Virtually all European languages (with the exception of Finnish, Hungarian and Basque) are part of the Indo-European group, and consequently contain a number of words which are similar in both sound and meaning. For example the words for father: German 'vater', Latin 'pater', French 'pere', Italian and Spanish 'padre'.

A knowledge of Latin is of enormous help in understanding all the Romance languages, in which many of the words are similar. The Latin word for 'love' is 'amor'. Related to 'love' in the English language is the word 'amorous' which means inclined to love; in love; and of or pertaining to love—the links are obvious. Similarly we have the Latin word for 'god': 'Deus'. In English the words Deity and Deify mean respectively 'divine status; a god; the Creator' and 'to make a god of '.

French was derived from the vulgar speech of the Roman legionaries, who called a head 'testa', a crockery shard, hence 'tete', and the shoulder 'spatular', a small spade, hence 'epaule', etc. About fifty per cent of ordinary English speech is derived either directly from Latin (+ Greek) or by way of Norman French, leading to many direct analogies between French and English.

As well as language similarities based on language grouping, foreign words can be remembered in a manner similar to that explained for remembering English words. As we are discussing French, the following two examples are appropriate: In French the word for 'book' is 'livre'. This can be remembered more readily if you think of the first four letters of the word 'library' which is a place where books are classified and studied. The French word for 'pen' is 'plume' which in English refers to a bird's feather, especially a large one used for ornament. This immediately brings to mind the quill pen used widely before the invention of the steel nib, fountain pen and biro. The link-chain 'plume—feather—quill—pen' will make the remembering of the French word a simple task.

Apart from the Latin, Greek, and French, the rest of English is largely Anglo-Saxon, going back to German, giving rise to countless words that are virtually the same in German and English—glass, grass, will, hand, arm, bank, halt, wolf, etc. while others are closely related, light (licht), night (nacht), book (buch), stick (stock) and follow (folgen).

Learning languages, both our own and those of other people's, need not be the frustrating and depressing experience it so often is. It is simply a matter of organising the information you have to learn in such a way as to enable your memory to 'hook on' to every available scrap of information.

The methods outlined in this chapter should give you a solid basis for becoming more proficient in the various languages, and for *enjoying* the process of becoming more efficient.

CHAPTER TWENTY

REMEMBERING FOR EXAMINATIONS

Few people hear the word 'examination' without a slight feeling of fear or distaste. In *Speed Reading*, I have dealt comprehensively with methods for studying three to ten times more effectively. Here I'm going to discuss examinations in relation to memory systems.

Typically, the person taking an examination dashes to his seat in order to use all the available time and reads his examination paper so nervously, quickly and confusedly that he has to read it over again to find out just what it is he is being asked.

At this stage he usually becomes flustered, desperately trying to co-ordinate all the information which he thinks might relate to the question he is trying to answer, but which is buried in the mire of all his other disorganised knowledge. How often have you yourself, or have you seen someone else write an examination, spending as much as 15 minutes of an hour's time jotting down notes, scratching his head, resting his chin on his hand, and frowning as he frantically tries to recall all that he knows and yet at this moment does *not* know?

Such students often possess more knowledge about the subject than others. I remember at least three students in my undergraduate years who knew more about certain subjects than virtually everyone in the class and who used to give private tuition and coaching to those who were struggling.

Extraordinarily and regularly, these students would fail to excel at examination time, invariably complaining that they had not had time in the examination room to gather together the knowledge they had.

Problems such as theirs can be overcome by preparing for examinations using the Major and Skipnum Memory Systems, in conjunction with the link system.

Let us assume that the subject to be examined is psychology. Reviewing your notes, you realise that in the year's study you have covered four major areas, and that each area had four or five main theories, four or five major figures, and a number of experiments.

Applying this information to the memory system, you link the name of the first major area with the first word of the system, list the main theories on the following numbers, the main figures on the next numbers and after that the experiments. For the next major area you repeat this process until you have covered the major key words and ideas for the content of the year's course. Should any of these items have smaller items which you think might be significant, they can be linked to the key psychology words.

It may surprise you to learn that in circumstances where my students have applied these systems, their memory list for any given subject in a yearly exam seldom exceeds 70 items! In the examination room they are immediately far ahead of their erstwhile peers. When considering their answers to questions, they simply survey their organised knowledge in less than a minute, selecting those items that are relevant. In addition, the items selected are already in an 'essay' form.

In the example we are using, the answer to any question could take the following form 'in considering the problem of blank and blank I wish to discuss three of the major areas of psychology, citing the theories of blank from the second, and the theories of blank and blank from the third area. In connection with these areas and theories I will also consider the importance of the following major figures in the history of these ideas, and shall discuss in relation to the entire question the following experiments: . . .'

Without having said *anything* our imaginary student already sounds well on the way to a 1st class! Indeed he may well be, for as his initial fact getting-down task has been made so much more easy, the amount of time left to him for creative discussion and comment on what he has written will be greater.

To carry this last point a little further—it is advisable to peg on to your memory system creative or original ideas that flash into your mind concerning the subject of examination. These often make the difference between a 1st and 2nd class, yet normally they tend either to get mixed up in a generally confused presentation of knowledge and ideas or lost in the heat of the moment.

Smaller details, including the titles of books, articles and dates, can obviously be co-ordinated with the system explained above.

Examinations are *not* all that difficult. Explaining what you know in an organised and coherent fashion to an examiner can be—use your memory systems to help you.

CHAPTER TWENTY-ONE

REMEMBER TO REMEMBER!

You have now completed your basic course and should have learnt no fewer than twenty different systems for remembering different items!

After being given a rough historical context within which to work, you were given an initial memory test designed to establish the limits of your memory at that time.

The first chapters (in an attempt to overcome as rapidly as possible the deficiencies laid bare by the test.) dealt with the basic principles of remembering, giving you practice in the rules of exaggeration, movement, substitution and absurdity. The principles learnt in these systems were then applied to the new memory system of Heinz Norden, Skipnum, and to the Major System.

From the Major System you were able to branch out into the remembering of numbers, anniversaries, birthdays and historical dates, including the year, month and day.

Apart from this you learnt systems for remembering names and faces, speeches, jokes, narratives, articles, languages, and playing cards.

With the information you now possess you are ready to use your memory in a far more adequate and comprehensive way. Apart from your business and social life many of the systems may be used to give 'memory demonstrations' ranging from reeling off lists of items to picking out the 'missing cards' from a deck.

Building a good memory is much like growing up. You develop a little day by day but seldom notice the changes until you suddenly look back at yourself, often through other people's eyes, writing or photographs. You may not even now be fully aware of the strides you have made during your reading of *Speed Memory*.

To see just how far you *have* come, go back and look at the 'photograph' of your memory as recorded in the initial memory test. Things which at that time appeared (and were!) difficult will now seem like child's play.

We have come to the end of the course, but in a sense it is only a beginning. At the moment you are using abstract systems to remember items that have given you difficulty in the past. By continuing to use these systems and *actively* concerning yourself with *remembering to remember*, you will find that the systems themselves will become unnecessary, and that through the process of consciously working to improve your memory with 'artificial aids', you will have helped it to become vigorous and independent.

If you feel you have benefited from reading this book why not invest in a copy of Tony Buzan's SPEED READING also published by David & Charles.

To anyone reaching a reading speed of 350 words per minute plus 50 per cent comprehension of SPEED READING the author offers a £5 reduction in an ADVANCED READING COURSE taught personally by Tony Buzan.

For further details please write or telephone:

The Learning Methods Group,
84 Hampstead Way,
London NW11
01-455 8266.